BOEING

737-300 to 800

BOEING
737-300 to 800

Robbie Shaw

MBI Publishing Company

Library of Congress Cataloging-in-Publication Data available

ISBN 0-7603-0699-0

Printed in Singapore

A Note from the Author

The difficulty in continuing a series approach when dealing
with the world's best-selling airliner — albeit without its
earliest forms — is enormous. There are just so many customers and aircraft involved that the comprehensive treatment
allowed a less commercially successful aircraft — such as the
TriStar or DC-10 — is impossible. I have, therefore, left much
of detailed design history and technical specification to a later
series title on the 737-100 and -200 family.

Acknowledgements

I would like to thank a number of people for their valued
support during the project, in particular my good friend Iain
'McEwan' Logan, Matthew Martin, and Jeff and Ryan in
Seattle. A big thank you to Michael and Julie at the Boeing
New Bureau in London — I only wish that Boeing in the US
had been half as helpful: it's a lot easier to write a good book if
you can visit the locations. Finally, special thanks must go to
my wife Eileen, who not only endured endless hours of my
absence both in front of a word processor and in other parts of
the world armed with a camera, but also proof read everything.

All photographs, unless specifically credited otherwise, are
by the author.

Southwest Airlines has been a phenomenal success story. It is the largest operator
of the -300 with 190 of the type in use, some of which are painted in special colours
of US states served by the airline, including (as here) N383SW *Arizona One.*

CONTENTS

1 INTRODUCTION AND EVOLUTION

On 19 February 1990 the Boeing 737 entered the record books when it became the best-selling airliner in the world. The actual aircraft that broke the record, a series -300 destined for British Midland Airways, was rolled out of the production hangar at Boeing's Renton plant. This was the 1,833rd 737 built, displacing the Boeing 727 tri-jet from its title of the world's most successful airliner.

The decision to build the 737 short-range transport jet was announced by Boeing on 19 February 1965, 25 years to the day before the record breaking achievement described above. Unlike its twin-engined T-tailed competitors, the BAC 1-11 (which had already flown) and the DC-9, Boeing decided on a conventional tail unit with the engines in pods under each wing.

The first customer for the 737 was the Federal German carrier Lufthansa — the first time a foreign airline had been the launch customer for a US airliner. This variant of the 737 was designated the series -100, with a capacity of 100 passengers and powered by two Pratt & Whitney JT8D-1 engines. The prototype took to the air for the first time on 9 April 1967, with deliveries commencing in December of that year. However only 30 series -100s were built, as the larger series -200 soon became the standard variant.

Before the prototype had even flown Boeing had already announced plans for a larger and more powerful variant, the series -200. The fuselage was lengthened by 6ft (1.82m) to accommodate up to 130 passengers, while improved JT8D engines gave an additional 10 percent thrust. Launch customer for this variant — and the first US airline to order the 737 — was United Airlines who ordered an initial batch of 40 aircraft. To demonstrate how quickly Boeing introduced production of the -200 United took delivery of its first -200 only two days after Lufthansa had taken delivery of its first series -100 aircraft. Although initially sales of the 737 were slower than expected, Boeing had faith in their product and announced the -200C and QC. These were the Convertible and Quick Change variants, featuring a large cargo door in the forward port fuselage. On the Quick Change variant seats are loaded on a pallet rather than removed and loaded by row.

The first variant flew in September 1968 and was delivered to Wien Alaska Airlines soon afterwards. Over the next two decades the -200 sold in large numbers, particularly when the -200 Advanced was introduced, featuring the use of graphite composites to reduce the weight of the airframe, thereby increasing the maximum payload. The last of the 1,114 737-200s built was delivered to China in August 1988. Of these, 19 were equipped as navigation trainers for the USAF with the designation T-43A, while three special surveillance variants were acquired by the Indonesian Air Force.

ABOVE: Aer Lingus has operated four different variants of the 737 — the -200, -300, -400 and -500. Only the latter two are now in service with the airline, with the -400s used predominantly on the high density Heathrow–Dublin route. Aer Lingus adopted a slightly revised livery in 1996 — strangely enough very soon after it received a large amount of state aid. Displaying the new livery on approach to Heathrow is 737-448 EI-BXB *St. Call.*

LEFT: Any visitor to Renton will see an airfield littered with numerous 'green' 737s in primer in the final stages of preparation for their maiden flight. Most, if not all, will wear the same registration — N1786B — the only clue to the eventual customer being the fully painted rudder. Those who know their airline liveries will recognise that the aircraft in this photograph is destined for China Southwest Airlines.

Capitalising on the amazing success of the 737, Boeing's design department worked hard to update the aircraft, the result of which was the introduction of the 'new generation' -300, -400 and -500. The go-ahead for the 737-300 was given in March 1981 following orders from USAir and Southwest Airlines for 10 aircraft each with options for a further 20. The engines chosen for the 'new generation' 737s were CFM56s which are not only more powerful, but considerably quieter than those used on the earlier variants. All three models have a common wing span with a slight increase on the -200, while the overall height is reduced by 6in (15cm). The fuselage of the 737-300 has been increased by 9ft 5in (2.87m) giving a typical mixed capacity of 128 passengers, up to a maximum capacity of 149. These three variants have common two-man cockpits featuring improved avionics, and all five variants have identical fuselage width and height.

The maiden flight of the first series -300 was on 24 February 1984, and soon afterwards Piedmont ordered 15 of the type. The popularity of the new type became evident when the 737-300 chalked up yet another record for Boeing in 1985 — amassing orders for 252 aircraft during that year. The -300 is likely to be the best selling of all 737 variants with 1,096 ordered to date, just 14 short of the total for the series -200.

The introduction of the series -400 brought an even greater fuselage stretch by a further 10ft (3.45m) which, in mixed seating configuration, can carry 146 passengers, a number which can be increased to 170 in all-economy or charter configuration. The -400 proved to be a winner from the start, with an order for 25 from Piedmont, plus the first of many orders from the increasing number of aircraft leasing companies. The 1,000th 'new generation' 737 built was the first -400 for British

Airways, and was delivered to the airline on 16 October 1991.

By the mid-1980s, although still popular, the series -200 was a 25-year old design and, compared with the technology of the -300, was becoming outdated. However, research showed that airlines still wanted an aircraft the size and capacity of the -200 — the obvious solution was to produce a 'new generation' -200, hence the -500 was born. The type was launched in May 1987, and promised to be 25 percent more fuel efficient than the elderly -200s. The prototype -500 took off from Renton on its maiden flight on 30 June 1989. The first production -500 variant was delivered to Southwest on 28 February the following year, by which time 193 had been ordered by 19 airlines.

An important milestone in the career of the Boeing 737 and Lufthansa occurred on 25 February 1991 when the 2,000th 737 built was handed over to the German airline. Coincidentally, this was the 100th 737 Lufthansa had taken delivery of over a period of 23 years. The year 1991 was a boom time for both the airlines and therefore the manufacturers. During that year Boeing delivered a total of 215 737s, setting yet another record — this time for the most commercial aircraft of a single type to be delivered in a year.

25 YEARS ON

A quarter of a century after the first 737 flew demand for the 737 family was still strong, however Airbus Industrie and its popular A320 was certainly making inroads into much of what was Boeing's traditional market. The introduction of the A319 and A321 further enhanced the Airbus narrow-body family, and Boeing had to act decisively to head off its growing rival.

From the outset Boeing worked closely with prospective customers, and it became apparent that what they wanted was an updated series of 737 variants. These should offer increased payload, range, speed and better take-off performance, at the same time as maintaining the 737's dispatch reliability. The result was announced by Boeing on 17 November 1993 — the Boeing 737 Next Generation — although it was originally known as the 737X. This comprises three aircraft designated the -600, -700 and -800, equating to the current -500, -300 and -400 series respectively.

The new variants feature increased wing span and higher tail fin, whilst the wing area is increased by some 25 percent, providing a 30 percent increase in fuel capacity. Together with increased fuel performance this will, for the first time, enable the 737 to operate US transcontinental services, a major selling point in the battle for orders from US airlines. Unlike Airbus and its fly-by-wire control systems, Boeing is sticking with the conventional flying controls as used on the earlier 737s. Powerplants for all three variants are CFM56-7 engines, providing greater thrust than the CFM56-3 engines which power the series -300, -400 and -500. The manufacturer has also taken the opportunity to update the interior of the cabin, benefiting from its experience on the 777.

An extensive flight test programme was undertaken by no fewer than 10 aircraft from the three variants, comprising three series -600s, four -700s and three -800s. The first type to be produced was the series -700, which equated to the popular -300. Launch customer for the -700 series was Southwest Airlines, who ordered no fewer than 63 of the type in January 1994. Six months later Maersk Air became the European launch customer with an order for six. The 737-800 is a stretched version of the current -400 with the fuselage length increased by almost 10ft (3m). This variant was officially launched on 5 September 1994 at the Farnborough Air Show, with orders for 40 aircraft from four undisclosed customers. These have since been identified, and include German charter airlines Hapag Lloyd and Air Berlin.

The smallest of the Next Generation 737s is the -600, which equates in size to the -500. The launch customer for this variant is SAS (Scandinavian Airlines) with an order for 41 aircraft in March 1995. At the time — before Boeing's takeover of McDonnell Douglas — this was a major coup for Boeing as SAS was a major customer of Boeing's competitor.

THE NEXT GENERATION

On 21 November 1996 Boeing trumpeted another coup when American Airlines announced a multi-million dollar deal to acquire and place options on a number of aircraft, including 75 Next Generation 737s. American also obtained 'purchase rights' to acquire a further 425 737s, which is quite amazing considering that the airline currently does not operate the 737. This order brought the total Next Generation 737 order book to an amazing 501 aircraft from 21 customers — before the first of the type had even flown! Four months later Boeing signed a similar deal with Delta Airlines, then with Continental Airlines likewise in the summer of 1997.

In July 1996 Boeing formed a new subsidiary, Boeing Business Jets, in a joint venture with General Electric. This was to market a version of the Next Generation 737 aimed specifically at the business jet market. This aircraft will be a high performance derivative of the 737-700, featuring the -700's fuselage with the wings and landing gear of the -800. With its excellent performance and range, allied with a spacious interior, the company views the 737 Business Jet as an ideal contender in a market dominated by types such as the Gulfstream and Dassault Falcon. Boeing also announced at the 1997 Paris Air Show that it was looking at three new variants of the Next Generation 737; later, in November 1997, it announced the launch of the -900 series with an order for 10 by Air Alaska.

The first Next Generation 737 was rolled out on 8 December 1996. This, the first series -700, was the 2,843rd 737 built and took to the air on its maiden flight on 9 February 1997. The prototype of the second member of the Next Generation family, the -800 was rolled out on 30 June 1997 with the first flight on the last day of following month. Roll out of the first -600 was planned for December 1997 with a maiden flight a month later and first deliveries to SAS in the late 1998.

The sales figures for the Next Generation 737 have been outstanding. After the 1997 Paris Air Show, by which date three 737-700s had flown but none had been delivered to customers, and the roll out of the -800 was imminent, a total of 627 aircraft had been ordered by 29 customers. Due to this phenomenal success Boeing announced increased production rates for the 737 — not just once, but thrice! By the second quarter of 1998 the production rate was due to reach 24 aircraft per month, the highest rate ever.

When Boeing launched the 737 programme 32 years ago it envisaged sales of around 600 aircraft. At the time of writing that figure has been oversubscribed by over 3,000! As an interesting aside, the prototype Boeing 737-100 was recently retired to the Museum of Flight at Boeing Field, 30 years 5 months and 12 days after its maiden flight. It had spent the last 26 years in service with NASA in the test and research role.

The success of the Next Generation 737s can be summed up simply — they can fly higher, faster, farther and with lower operating and maintenance costs.

ABOVE RIGHT: The DC-9 proved to be the major competitor to the 737, and was itself built in significant numbers — 976 in total. All but 100 or so of these remain in use, primarily in North and South America. Like the 737, the DC-9 family was extended with the introduction of the MD-80 series, through to the MD-90 and its MD-95 (now the Boeing 717) follow-up. TWA still operates a sizeable fleet of elderly DC-9s alongside increasing numbers of MD-80s.

RIGHT: Rotate! It is 09.00 Pacific Time on 31 July 1997 and prototype 737-800 N737BX lifts off from Renton's runway on its maiden flight. *Boeing*

2 DESIGN

Although the 737 had already proved an unqualified success, the concept of the series -300 was basically to improve on what was already on offer. Put simply, the plan was to increase the size, and therefore the capacity, as well as range, while using more powerful yet quieter and more fuel-efficient engines. This was a tall order indeed, but one which Boeing's designers fulfilled admirably, producing the most popular of all 737 variants.

There are many reasons for the success of the series -200, such as its reliability and a performance which enables it to operate into small airports with short runways. Leading and trailing edge devices and a very effective reverse thrust mechanism were instrumental in reducing the approach speed and landing roll to enable the type to operate into smaller airfields. The height of the lower fuselage above the ground proved ideal for loading and maintenance teams to access various doors and panels, enabling speedy turn-round times. Also, the cabin dimensions — the same as 707 and 727 models — had proved a good selling point for fleet commonalty for some customers. Naturally, the designers wanted to change as few of these positive aspects as possible.

To cater for the increase in capacity, the series -300 has fuselage plugs immediately forward of the wing root and behind the trailing edge, amounting to 9ft 5in (2.87m). The horizontal tailplanes received a slight extension, while the leading edge of the vertical fin was extended forwards at it base, though the height was actually reduced by 6in (15cm). The wing span was increased slightly by 1ft 9in (53cm), as well as being strengthened to cope with the heavier engines. To counter possible flutter effects (due to the more powerful engines) weighted probes were designed to be fitted to each wingtip, though in the end these devices were not required. To reduce the approach speed caused by the increase in weight, the leading edge slat was extended from the engine pylon to the wingtip, this also resulted in an increase in the maximum cruising altitude, further improving fuel efficiency.

The most daunting task facing the designers was the engine location. On the -200 there was concern that the underslung engines would literally be a magnet for Foreign Object Damage (FOD) whereby stones and other debris would be sucked into the intake and damage the fan blades. Fortunately these fears proved groundless, though a deflector was fitted to the nosewheel and dissipaters under the nacelles on aircraft operated by airlines who operate the type into rough strips. Without going into technical detail, the best way to reduce engine noise is to increase the intake diameter. This is one reason why the CFM engine was quieter than the Pratt & Whitney used on the -200.

As the CFM56 engine was selected to power the -300 Boeing's designers had their work cut out to fit it without extensive and expensive modifications to the new model. There were alternatives of course, a major redesign of the wing, or increasing the length of the undercarriage legs; though neither option was going to be popular with either Boeing or the customers.

Boeing worked hard with CFM International to overcome the problems, and overcome they were. Producing 20,100lb (89.38kN) thrust the CFM56-3B-1 was the engine selected to power the 737-300. First ground runs were undertaken in March 1982, with flight testing aboard a Boeing 707 test aircraft from Edwards AFB commencing 11 months later. Subsequently the uprated CFM56-3B-2 producing 22,100lb (98.27kN) was made available. To improve ground clearance, the engine accessory drive gearbox and transfer gearbox were relocated from the bottom to the side of the engine, allowing the nacelle to have a flattened rather than oval underside. This helped considerably in relation to ground clearance, but it was still not enough. The cure was to hang the engine nacelle from a pylon, with the pylon literally wrapped around the wing so that the nacelle was forward of, rather than slung underneath, the wing. Coupled with a lengthened and slightly repositioned nosewheel leg there was now ample ground clearance.

The -300 featured a whole host of other improvements over the -200, though these were all internal. Taking advantage of components developed for the Boeing 757 new light weight but larger overhead stowage bins and improved cabin lighting were introduced. Electronic flight instruments were also made available to customers who specified such a fit — which Trans Australian Airlines was the first to do.

The prototype 737-300 was rolled out at Renton on 17 January 1984, taking to the air on 24 February, eight days ahead of schedule. This was the 1,001st 737 built, and wore the registration N73700 during this inaugural flight with Jim McRoberts at the controls. The prototype and first two produc-

TOP RIGHT: Shenzhen Airlines is one of the many Chinese operators of the 737. Based at Shenzhen — a mere stone's throw across the border from the Special Administrative Region of Hong Kong— the airline has a fleet of six leased 737-300s, including B-2940 seen here taxying to the gate at Beijing's Capital airport.

CENTRE RIGHT: British Airways Gatwick-based 737 fleet continues to grow and grow, and now numbers 8 -200s and 25 -400s. The airline's fleet at Gatwick now numbers nearly 70 aircraft. Many will be surprised to know that the airline actually serves more destinations from Gatwick than from Heathrow. Photographed as it rotates is 737-436 G-DOCS *River Teifi*.

RIGHT: Estonian Air is the national carrier of the small Baltic country which is emerging strongly since its independence from the Soviet Union. In a bold move the airline decided to dispose of the fleet of Yak-40s and Tu-134s inherited from the former Aeroflot regional division. Instead they leased two new 737-500s in June 1995 and February 1996 from ILFC. These have since been joined by a pair of Fokker 50s. Photographed at Gatwick at the completion of a flight from Tallinn is 737-5Q8 ES-ABD.

tion examples undertook a nine month long certification programme from Boeing Field. In airline service the series -300 usually seats around 128 passengers in a mixed cabin configuration, though a maximum of 149 can be carried.

Following on from the success of the -300 Boeing's designers came up with the larger -400, though competitors doubted that additional growth could be accommodated without a major and expensive redesign. The -400 featured a fuselage increased in length by 10ft (3m); this increased the passenger load to about 146 in mixed configuration, and up to 170 in an all-economy fit, the latter being favoured by some charter operators. This increase in capacity required additional overwing exits to satisfy safety requirements.

The -400 was Boeing's answer to fill a gap between the 737-300 and the 757, a gap which Airbus Industrie was filling with its popular A320. For commonalty all other external dimensions were the same as the series -300. A tail bumper was fitted to counter any possible tailscrapes during rotation as this had already occurred several times in the early operations of the 757. To cope with the increased weight the wing spar was strengthened, while an additional spoiler was fitted to each wing to assist deceleration. Then, bowing to customer pressure Boeing fitted as standard full 'glass cockpit' avionics with EFIS displays, this meant that the -400 had a very similar cockpit layout to the 757/767, though not similar enough when compared to Airbus types whose pilots can obtain a common type rating enabling them to fly more than one type without retraining. The prototype -400 was rolled out on 26 January 1988, the same day as the roll-out of the first 747-400. The first flight was on 19 February 1988, again the registration N73700 was applied, and again Jim McRoberts was in command of the aircraft. Two aircraft were involved in the seven month long 500 hour plus flight test programme to satisfy the certification process.

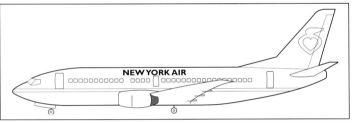

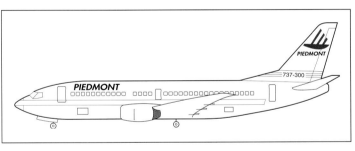

TOP: For the last few years Norway's Braathens has painted an aircraft in special 'Sommerflyet' markings. 737-505 LNBRJ has been the aircraft chosen in most cases, and in 1995 featured a particularly colourful children's drawings on the fuselage.

CENTRE: A subsidiary of Texas Air, New York Air began services in December 1980 between New York and Washington, initially with DC-9 aircraft. The airline quickly built up a network down America's East Coast, adding MD-82s to its inventory. In August 1985 the airline took delivery of its first Boeing 737-300s, however, in February 1987 the airline was merged with Continental Airlines. New York Air's distinctive red and white livery included a white 'big apple' on the fin.

ABOVE: Piedmont Airlines operated a vast jet fleet of Boeing 727s, 737s and Fokker F-28s on its routes throughout the eastern US with major hubs at Baltimore, Charlotte and Dayton. In 1987 it was taken over by USAir, enhancing the latter's fleet inventory considerably. The 737-400s on order were delivered to USAir.

LEFT: Speculation about the rudder on the 737 has been rife after accidents in which the cause has yet to be determined but suspicion points to the rudder. The 'Big Foot' marking on the tail of this British Airways 737-400 (G-DOCS) however has nothing to do with the rudder. It was painted this way for Christmas 1996 to highlight a charity fund raising event by the airline's Gatwick based cabin crew to deliver presents to deprived children in Bulgaria.

THE 'BABY' 737-500

The new generation 737s were proving popular with customers and the order book continued to grow. It became apparent however that for some operators of the 737-200 the series -300 and -400 were really too big for their needs, but they wanted a -200 with the qualities of the newer types, particularly as regards to fuel efficiency. Boeing's answer was the series -500, a type with all the attributes of the -300 and -400 but dimensions of the -200.

Initially the manufacturer intended to designate this series -1000, but later changed to the more logical -500. This 'baby' new generation aircraft features a fuselage length just 1ft 7in (47cm) longer than the -200, but with a wing span and height common to its cousins, the -300 and -400. This slight increase in length offers a maximum capacity of 132 passengers.

Both electronic and conventional electro-mechanical cockpits were made available for the customer to choose their preferred option. The standard powerplant was the same CFM56-3-B1 as used on the -300, though a derated CFM56-3-B4 with 18,500lb (82.29kN) is also available for customers. Production of the series -200 ceased in August 1988, however the -500 was poised to fill the void and took to the air for the first time on 30 June 1989. Again Jim McRoberts was in command of the aircraft and, surprise surprise, the now famous N73700 markings were applied. This was the sole aircraft used in the 375-hour seven month long flight test and certification programme. Series -200 customers who have purchased the -500 are no doubt delighted that the newcomer is 25 percent more fuel-efficient than its older stablemate.

THE NEXT GENERATION -600, -700, -800

Following on from the successful new generation series of 737s is the Next Generation, originally dubbed the 737X. The Next Generation family comprises three models ; the -600, -700 and -800, which equate to the -500, -300 and -400 respectively. All three models will be powered by the CFM56-7B, albeit at a different thrust settings for each model. Those powering the -600 will be rated at 22,000lb (97.9kN), 24,000lb (106.8kN) for the -700 and 26,200lb (116.6kN) for the -800. These engines will enable the type to fly faster and further than previous 737s with less noise and fewer emissions. Noise on the ground will also be reduced thanks to a new diffuser duct and cooling vent silencer on the Auxiliary Power Unit (APU).

All three variants will have a common wing span increased considerably over the earlier series by 17ft 8in (5.43m), with the fin height increased correspondingly. More importantly the wing area is increased by 25 percent to 1,340sq ft (125sq m), enabling 30 percent more fuel to be carried and considerably enhancing the range. This increase in range is almost 900nm greater than current models, permitting US transcontinental flights for the first time. Perhaps surprisingly the manufacturer is staying with conventional flying control systems rather than the fly-by-wire system used by their competitor Airbus. Further cabin interior updates are featured, this time drawing on experience gained in the construction of the 777, whereby lighter materials are used yet giving more overhead storage capacity per passenger.

As usual the customer will have the choice of cabin configuration which, in the -600 will range from 108 in mixed class to 132 in all-economy fit. For the -700 these figures are from 128 to 149, while the larger -800 can seat from 162 to 189.

THE BUSINESS JET

Boeing is also offering a Business Jet derivative of the -700 fitted with auxiliary fuel tanks offering a range in excess of 6,200nm (11,480km) permitting intercontinental sectors such as London–Johannesburg and New York–Tokyo to be undertaken. Also the spacious cabin will allow a customer to specify interior fittings to order, ranging from office and conference facilities to private suites with shower facilities. The Boeing Business Jet (BBJ) features the fuselage of the -700 but with the strengthened wing and undercarriage of the -800. To improve its appeal to prospective customers the manufacturer is looking at increasing the maximum speed from Mach 0.82 to 0.84. It would also like to raise the operating ceiling from 41,000ft to 43,000ft (12,497m to 13,106m) which would be of enormous benefit in reducing delays in congested skies if their aircraft could fly higher than any other commercial airliner. By September 1997 Boeing had taken 25 orders for the BBJ, with the first delivery scheduled for September 1998.

At the 1997 Paris Air Show Boeing announced that it was also looking at no less than three new variants of the Next Generation 737 — before the first such aircraft had even been delivered! These would include the -700X, based on the Business Jet but with the range increased by up to 865nm (1,600km), even fully loaded. Also based on the Business Jet would be the Quick Change (QC) passenger/cargo variant with a large side cargo door. This would form the basis of Boeing's bid for a US Navy contract to replace the C-9 Skytrain passenger/cargo transport. This seemed to be a prudent move, which paid off early in September 1997 when the US Navy ordered two of the variant, with repeat orders likely. Finally there is the -900X. This would be a stretched version of the -800 with fuselage plugs forward and aft of the wing increasing the fuselage length by 7ft 10in (2.4m) which, in a two class cabin configuration would increase capacity by 18 passengers.

737-700

The prototype 737-700 was rolled out on 8 December 1996, the following day Boeing's Renton factory came to a standstill when the new plane took to the air on its maiden flight. This time the favoured N73700 registration was dispensed with in favour of N737X. The pilots for this inaugural flight were Mike Hewett and Ken Higgins, and after a three hour 35 minute flight they landed at nearby Boeing Field. On stepping down from the aircraft Hewett was obviously delighted, commenting:

"We've got a winner! This plane is fantastic, I think 737 pilots around the world are going to feel right at home in this cockpit".

A further three -700s joined the flight test programme, as did three -600s and three -800s. The maiden flight of the first -800 was on 31 July 1997 with Mike Hewett and Jim McRoberts at

ABOVE: The CFM-56-3 engine powers the 737 new generation series aircraft. To give adequate ground clearance however, the Boeing design team had to change the way of mounting the engine. Unlike the -200 where the engine is hung on a pod underneath the wing, the engine mount on the new generation series is wrapped around the leading edge of the wing. Similarly, the engine's designers changed the engine casing to an oval shape and repositioned some components. These changes provide adequate ground clearance — but only just — as this photograph of a Southwest Airlines -300 shows.

the controls for the three hour five minute long test which was reported as flawless. The prototype -600 was scheduled to take to the air in January 1998; all went ahead well and on 18 August 1998 the FAA granted type certification to the Next Generation 737-600. On 18 September launch customer SAS took delivery of the first plane out of their order for 55 737-600s.

In high density configuration the 737-800 seats nine passengers more than the A320, and this no doubt was a factor when the German charter carriers Air Berlin, Germania and Hapag-Lloyd selected the Boeing product. The US FAA has awarded certification of Next Generation 737s under 'grandfather rights' where they are treated as variants of previous 737 models. The European Joint Aviation Authorities (JAA) however are more reticent, stating that the current emergency exit procedures do not meet the Joint Aviation Requirements (JAR) specifications, and until they do seating capacity should be restricted to a maximum of 180.

Boeing has responded by proposing to fit new Type III exits which feature an automatic fast opening mechanism which is easier to operate by passengers, and can be opened in just three seconds as opposed to the 13 seconds required by the Authorities. The new exit door differs from previous types in that it hinges outwards and upwards, but still remaining attached to the airframe. The new exit will be fitted as standard from the 26th aircraft onwards, and will be retrofitted to those

aircraft delivered to European customers prior to this. It is likely this proposal will be accepted, allowing the manufacturer to seat up to 189 on the -800 as advertised, though by mid October 1997 the manufacturer was still waiting to hear from the JAA.

The first -700 was due to have been certified by September 1997, however this was delayed until 7 November because of late structural and control systems modifications and continuing evaluation by the JAA. During flight testing it was found that at high speed the horizontal stabiliser was suffering from unacceptably high levels of in-spar rib vibration. To counter this there is a modification to stiffen the stabiliser by adding a composite panel to the trailing edge spar. This modification will also be standard on the series -800, as will late changes to the lateral control system. The US FAA gave type certification clearing the 737-800 for passenger service within the United States on 13 March 1998, only one month later than hoped.

3 PRODUCTION

THE FACTORIES

The Boeing Commercial Airplane Company has its headquarters in Seattle, Washington, and is without doubt the largest employer in the region. The headquarters itself is located at the company's Renton facility, one of three airfields the company operates from in the area. Fabrication work is undertaken at Boeing's Wichita, Kansas factory, a facility which is renowned predominantly for work on military types such as the C-135 and B-52. Much of the fuselage and wing, as well as thrust reversers, are manufactured here. Engine cowlings for the new generation variants are built by the Rohr Corporation in California.

North of Seattle is Boeing's Everett facility, built from scratch to produce the 747. There the 767 and 777 are assembled and tested. Back in the Seattle suburbs and only a few miles from Renton is Boeing Field for flight testing and pre-delivery inspection of all 737s and 757s. The paint shop here takes care of the majority of 737 external paintwork and company livery. Initially the 737 production and assembly line was located at Boeing Field, but in December 1970, after 271 aircraft had been completed, this was transferred to Renton.

Fuselages are now built at Wichita and shipped to Renton by rail where they join the assembly line for mating with the wings and landing gear. Each aircraft then moves along the final assembly line to have other components such as engines, avionics and interiors are fitted. For the series -300/-400/-500 aircraft the fuselage is shipped in two parts and joined together at Renton, however fuselages of the Next Generation series aircraft are joined together at Wichita and shipped to Renton as one unit. Initially most of the external paint work was carried out at Renton, but today most 737 external paintwork is completed at Boeing Field. When a completed 737 emerges from the Renton assembly line it is finished in a greenish-coloured layer of primer to prevent corrosion. The exception to this is the rudder, which is finished in customer livery prior to being fitted to the aircraft. This has something to do with the weighing of the aircraft which affects the trim. When an aircraft is finally rolled-out it undergoes a complete check of all systems and ground runs of the engines. When these have been completed satisfactorily the aircraft is ready to go for its first flight. As the aircraft climbs out of the compact Renton airfield on its maiden flight it will climb to medium level for a short air test, prior to landing at Boeing Field, just a few miles distant. Here the aircraft will be painted in full customer livery, and, if necessary any fine tuning of the aircraft and its systems will be undertaken before the customer signs for his new purchase.

NEW TECHNOLOGIES AND ECONOMIES

Since the inception of the Next Generation 737 programme Boeing has continued to work very closely with the customer airlines, during which time the various customers suggested no less than 350 changes, and to Boeing's great credit, the manufacturer has been able to accommodate all but ten of these.

The increasing sophistication of computer software has been

BELOW: This primer coloured 737-300 is destined for Southwest Airlines, and is seen lining-up on the runway at Renton. The aircraft will be fast-taxied up and down the runway two or three times and, once the pilots are satisfied everything appears normal, it will take-off never to return. The flight to nearby Boeing Field may last just a few minutes.

RIGHT: The first three series -800s in final assembly at Renton early in June 1997. The aircraft nearest the camera has a banner proclaiming 'Building on Success', 'First Boeing Next-Generation 737-800', 'Destined for Hapag-Lloyd'.

well utilised in the manufacturing and design phase, enabling the company to increase efficiency. This has also resulted in increased production line automation, particularly in the wing sections. Assembly of the fuselage at Wichita is now 97 percent undertaken by machines — this compares to 45 percent for the 737-300 fuselage. Automated spar assembly tools use electro-impulse riveters to stitch the wings together. These are undertaken in a renovated facility which many years ago built B-29s. Laser techniques are increasingly used when joining fuselage, wings and other major sections, eliminating shims. Lasers will also be used more extensively in the calibration of tools.

The Next Generation variants have an additional spoiler on each wing, while a new aluminium alloy is used for the wing upper skin. The leading edge devices have been simplified by using fewer parts, similarly the flap system has 37 percent fewer parts and 33 percent fewer bearings, leading to a reduction in weight and easier maintenance. As to the engine mounting, a simplified strut and easier access will reduce engine change times to less than six hours. Further weight saving has been achieved as over 4,000ft (1,219m) of wiring has been eliminated.

PRODUCTION RATE

Over the years production cycle time has steadily reduced from 15 months down to 10 months, however these improvements will enable Boeing to reduce this time even further, hopefully down to six months by the end of 1998.

On 24 February 1984 the 1,001st 737 - the prototype -300 took to the air. In February 1991 the 2,000th 737 was delivered to Lufthansa. In 1991 Boeing's 737 production line was working flat out during a boom time in the industry and the company delivered 215 of the type that year. However in the aftermath of the Gulf War the airline industry in the West was in serious recession, and the production rate was slashed accordingly. Even in the last quarter of 1996, when the industry had come through a couple of years of sustained growth, the 737 production rate was a mere eight and a half aircraft a month, or 102 per year.

As orders for the 737s, and other Boeing aircraft as well as Airbus types pour in, the Boeing Company intends to increase dramatically the production rate for the 737. By the third quarter of 1997 the company intended to produce 21 aircraft a month, meaning an amazing 252 per year. This figure could even double if Boeing decides, (as it has intimated it may do) to switch one of the two 757 production lines over to 737s. Indeed, in May 1997 the company announced a further increase in production to 24 aircraft a month by the second quarter of 1998. One of the 737 production lines will remain dedicated to production of the older series -300/-400/-500 until such time the demand from the customers ceases.

The company is, however, keeping open its options of moving the current production line of these aircraft into an adjacent building and take over one of the two 757 production lines, thereby enabling it to double production rates of the Next Generation aircraft. Recent events however have added another factor to the equation; with Boeing's recent acquisition of McDonnell-Douglas it is not inconceivable that it might wish to make better use of the under-utilised MD-80/MD-90 produc-

ABOVE LEFT: No fewer than 29 737 series -300, -400 and -500s are visible in this shot of the assembly line at Renton. Customers identified by the fully painted rudders include British Airways, Egyptair, Lufthansa, Southwest, Varig and VASP. *Boeing*

ABOVE: Braathens 737-505 LN-BRJ has worn a number of special 'Sommerflyet' markings in its lifetime. It's seen at Gatwick painted to celebrate the 1996 winter Olympics held in Lillehammer, Norway.

RIGHT: The upper surfaces of the 737-500 wing, showing the trailing edge flaps.

tion line at Long Beach and, who knows, Boeing may consider switching 757 production there.

One glitch in Boeing's plans for increased 737 production occurred in October 1997 when production was halted for 25 days due to parts' shortages by suppliers. Ultimately, this resulted in a shortfall of almost 10 Next Generation 737 deliveries by the end of 1997.

In front of 50,000 guests at Renton the first Next Generation 737 was rolled out on 8 December 1996. This, the first Series -700 was the 2,843rd 737 built and took to the air on its maiden flight on 9 February 1997, with the first delivery to Southwest Airlines scheduled for October 1997. In mid-February 1997 the fuselage for the prototype -800 left Wichita by railroad car for Renton, and the aircraft was rolled out on 30 June, with its maiden flight on 31 July 1997. This was the 2,906th 737 built. European certification was given on 19 February 1998 allowing Hapag-Lloyd to take delivery of its first -800 in March. Roll out of the first -600 had taken place on 8 December 1997 with its maiden flight a month later. First deliveries to launch customer SAS took place on 18 September 1998.

4 TECHNICAL SPECIFICATION

Series	-300	-400	-500
First flight date	24/2/84	19/2/88	30/6/89
Max. accommodation	149	170	132
Wing span	94ft 9in (28.88m)	94ft 9in (28.88m)	94ft 9in (28.88m)
Length	109ft 7in (33.4m)	119ft 7in (36.45m)	101ft 9in (31.0m)
Height	36ft 6in (11.13m)	36ft 6in (11.13m)	36ft 6in(11.13m)
Max. t/o weight	138,500lb (62,822kg)	150,000lb (68,040kg)	133,500lb (60,550kg)
Range at max. t/o wt	2,270nm (4,204km)	2,090nm (3,870km)	2,420nm (4,481km)
Cruising speed	Mach 0.745	Mach 0.745	Mach 0.745
Max. ceiling	37,000ft (11,278m)	37,000ft (11,278m)	37,000ft (11,278m)
Take-off distance	7,500ft (2,286m)	8,640ft (2,633m)	8,640ft (2,633m)
Landing distance	4,700ft (1,433m)	4,450ft (1,356m)	4,450ft (1,356m)

Series	-600	-700	-800
First flight date	Due January 1998	9 February 1997	31 July 1997
Max. accommodation	132	149	189
Wing span	112ft 7in (34.31m)	112ft 7in (34.31m)	112ft 7in (34.31m)
Length	102ft 6in(31.24m)	110ft 4in (33.63m)	129ft 6in (39.47m)
Height	41ft 3in (12.6m)	41ft 2in (12.56m)	41ft 2in (12.56m)
Max. t/o weight	144,500lb (65,574kg)	154,000lb (69,885kg)	172,500lb (78,244kg)
Range at max t/o wt.	3,717nm (5,981km)	3,245nm (6,009km)	2,930nm (5,246km)
Cruising speed	Mach 0.782	Mach 0.781	Mach 0.785
Max. ceiling	41,000ft (12,497m)	41,000ft (12,497m)	41,000ft (12,497m)
Take-off distance	6,160ft (1,877m)	6,700ft (2,042m)	7,600ft (2,316m)
Landing distance	4,160ft (1,268m)	4,450ft (1,356m)	5,250ft (1,600m)

Take-off and landing distances are quoted at maximum weight on a hard, dry runway at sea level.

Take-off data is calculated for air temperature of 86°F (30°C)

For all six variants the maximum speed is Mach 0.82.

ABOVE RIGHT: This diagram gives some idea of the size comparisons of the three Next Generation variants. The larger -800 (turquoise) is some 25 percent longer than the -600 (grey).

RIGHT: Maiden flight of the prototype 737-600 (N7376) was on 22 January 1998. The aircraft is seen here on a subsequent test flight from Boeing Field. This version is quite distinctive due to the stubby fuselage and tall fin, giving it a rather squat appearance

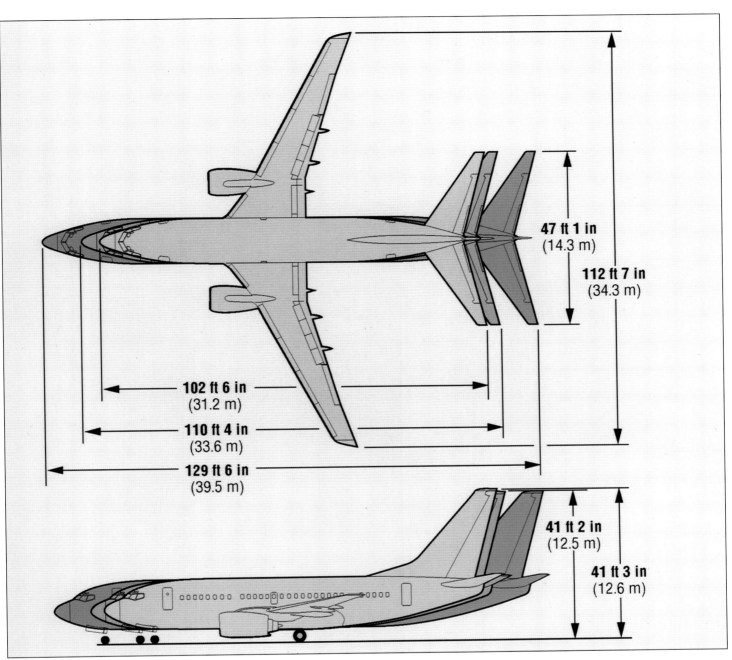

47 ft 1 in
(14.3 m)

112 ft 7 in
(34.3 m)

102 ft 6 in
(31.2 m)

110 ft 4 in
(33.6 m)

129 ft 6 in
(39.5 m)

41 ft 2 in
(12.5 m)

41 ft 3 in
(12.6 m)

The Next Generation 737s, namely the -300, -400 and -500 share the same cockpits with improved avionics and instrumentation when compared to the series -100 and -200. The cabin interiors are based on that developed for the 757, with contoured sidewall panels which permit the seat rows to be mounted one inch (2.54cm) further outboard than on previous models. This in turn increases the aisle width to 20in (50.8cm) from the previous 18in (45.7cm). In most cases this enables passengers to step around catering trolleys in the aisle and so ease congestion.

Although there is considerable commonality between all three models, it is the external differences which are most apparent, primarily size. When introduced, the 737-300 was the biggest variant and has subsequently become the best seller, at home on both short- and medium-range sectors, whether scheduled or inclusive tour charters. The maximum capacity is 149 passengers. The -300 was followed by the -400 which is noticeably longer. It is also easily identifiable by the twin overwing emergency exits, the only model to feature these until the introduction of the Series -800. The manufacturer was concerned that the increased length would increase the chance of a tail strike during rotation when operated by pilots with a lot of experience on the smaller models. To cater for this a tail bumper was fitted to protect the lower fuselage in the event of this happening. With increased capacity of up to a maximum of 170 passengers, the series -400 is much heavier than its predecessors, and requires longer take-off and landing distances. This increase in capacity has, not unnaturally, meant a slight reduction in range when compared to the -300.

The Series -500 was introduced due to customer demand for a more modern variant with similar capacity to the older variants, but with increased range, while being more frugal with fuel. The Series -500 seats from 108 to 132 and the fuselage dimensions differ only by a matter of inches when compared to the -200. The -500 has the greatest range of the new variants and lightly loaded can easily be operated from shorter runways. In its high gross weight version, however, it does require almost as much runway as the heavier -400. The -500 is an ideal aircraft for longer routes with thinner passenger demand, such as a mixed configuration for 108 passengers. Although smaller than the series -300, from many angles it can be difficult to differentiate between the two variants.

ABOVE RIGHT: A plan view of the 737-700 showing new technology wing whose leading edge devices consist of two flaps inboard, and four slats outboard of each engine. The wing gives an increase in area of 25 percent and fuel capacity by 30 percent compared to other variants. The increased span also features composite material ailerons and trim tab.

CENTRE RIGHT: The 3,000th 737, a Series -400 destined for Alaska Airlines, taxies out for its maiden flight at Renton.

RIGHT: The second 737-700 for Germania, seen in non-standard colours.

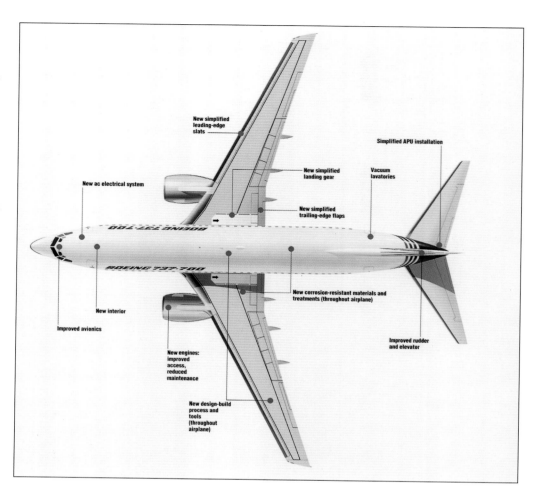

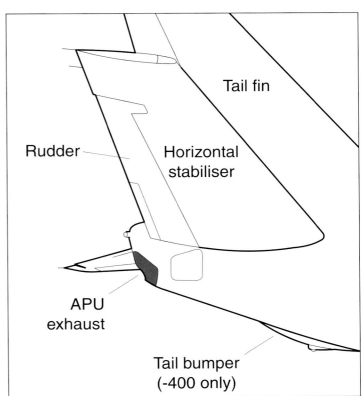

Tail fin

Rudder

Horizontal stabiliser

APU exhaust

Tail bumper (-400 only)

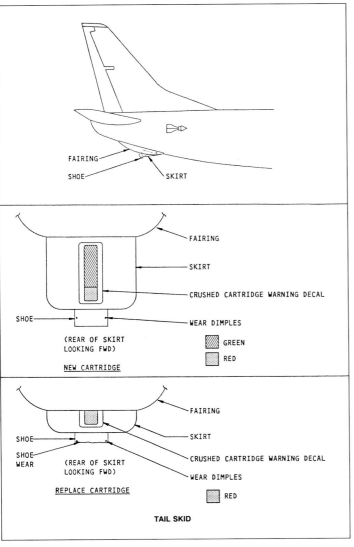

FAIRING

SHOE

SKIRT

FAIRING

SKIRT

CRUSHED CARTRIDGE WARNING DECAL

SHOE

WEAR DIMPLES

(REAR OF SKIRT LOOKING FWD)

GREEN

RED

NEW CARTRIDGE

FAIRING

SKIRT

SHOE

SHOE WEAR

CRUSHED CARTRIDGE WARNING DECAL

(REAR OF SKIRT LOOKING FWD)

WEAR DIMPLES

REPLACE CARTRIDGE

RED

TAIL SKID

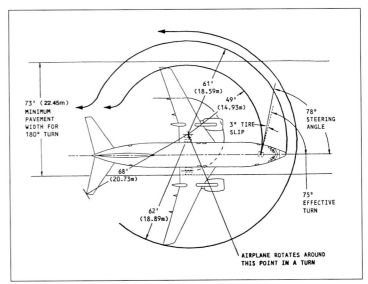

73' (22.45m) MINIMUM PAVEMENT WIDTH FOR 180° TURN

61' (18.59m)

49' (14.93m)

3° TIRE SLIP

78° STEERING ANGLE

68' (20.73m)

75° EFFECTIVE TURN

62' (18.89m)

AIRPLANE ROTATES AROUND THIS POINT IN A TURN

TOP LEFT: Because of increased production rates, space in the assembly hangars is at a premium and much of the finishing is done out of doors. This angle shows well the APU exhaust and tail assembly. How can you tell it's a -700 from this angle? The answer is one overwing exit, now modified to swing open outwards at the insistence of the European JAA.

TOP RIGHT: Sketch showing location of Auxiliary Power Unit (APU) exhaust, which is in the same location on all 737 models. It also shows the tail bumper fitted on the -400 to protect the underside of the fuselage in the event of this part of the aircraft coming into contact with the runway in case of over-rotation. Due to the increased length when compared to the -200 there were a small number of such incidents.

ABOVE: Ground manoeuvring capability of the 737-400.

LEFT: The 737-400 tail skid showing location and cartridge wear details. The skid prevented damage to the lower tail section in event of overrotation. The cartridge is made of honeycombed crushable material. It has a telltale which advances from green to red and the cartridge requires replacement once the red only shows.

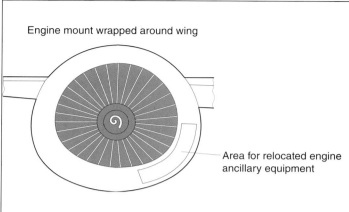

Engine mount wrapped around wing

Area for relocated engine ancillary equipment

ABOVE: The 737 has sturdy twin-wheel main undercarriage legs which retract inwards into the lower belly of the aircraft.

TOP LEFT: Head-on view of the CFM-56 engine and mounting. To give adequate ground clearance the engine casing was 'flattened' and some ancillary equipment relocated to the bulged part on the side of the engine. Similarly, the engine mounting is actually wrapped around the wing rather than suspended from it as in the -200.

ABOVE LEFT: The 737 nose cone hinges upwards to allow maintenance of the aircraft's weather radar.

FAR TOP LEFT AND FAR LEFT: The low-slung oval-shaped CFM-56 engine as used on the New and Next Generation series of aircraft.

LEFT AND BELOW: The 737 has baggage holds in the forward and rear fuselage. The inward-opening doors at head height are ideal for quick loading and unloading.

BOTTOM LEFT: Prototype Boeing 737-800 N737BX lands at Boeing Field at the cessation of yet another in the long series of certification test flights.

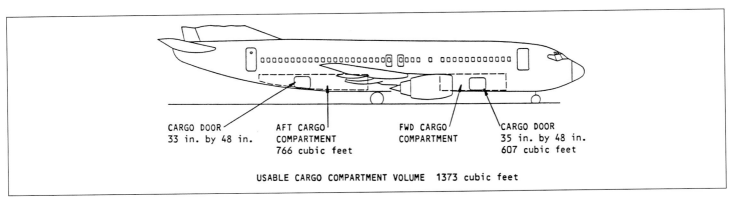

CARGO DOOR
33 in. by 48 in.

AFT CARGO
COMPARTMENT
766 cubic feet

FWD CARGO
COMPARTMENT

CARGO DOOR
35 in. by 48 in.
607 cubic feet

USABLE CARGO COMPARTMENT VOLUME 1373 cubic feet

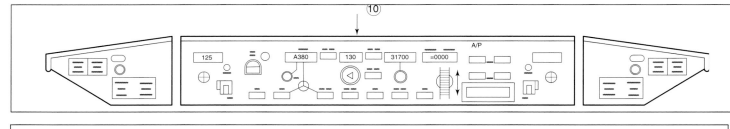

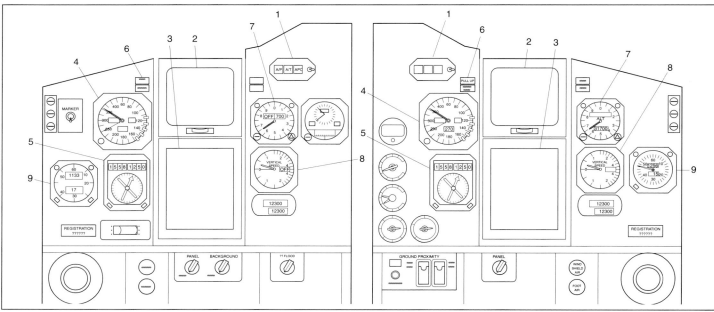

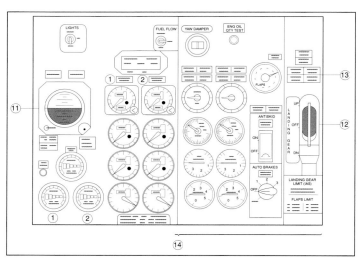

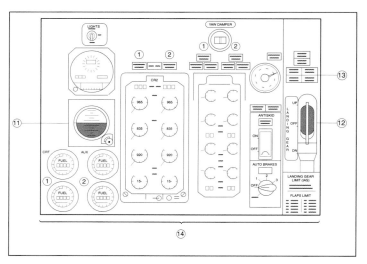

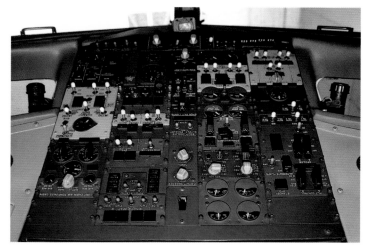

The cockpit instrument panels differ considerably between the 737 series. For example, take the centre instrument panel which is standard fit on the 737-400 (LEFT AND FAR LEFT). All the engine instruments are located here and the information is displayed in digital form. During the enquiry to the British Midland Kegworth crash it transpired that due to the severe vibration the crew had great difficulty trying to read the information on the engine instruments. As a result of this, British Airways specified anologue presentation of engine instruments for its 737-436 aircraft (LEFT). Compare the difference from that shown FAR LEFT.

Key numbers for instrument panel drawings:
1. Auto pilot on/off; 2. EFIS display — attitude displacement indicator; 3. EFIS display — horizontal situation indicator; 4. ASI — airspeed indicator; 5. ADF — autoatic direction finder; 6. GPWS — ground proximity warning system; 7. Altimeter; 8. VSI — vertical speed indicator; 9. Radar altimeter; 10. Auto-pilot control selector; 11. Secondary artificial horizon; 12. Landing gear lever; 13. Landing gear up/down indicator; 14. Engine temperature/pressure/power settings.

TOP LEFT: Glareshield instrument panel.

ABOVE LEFT: The Captain's and First Officer's instrument panels on the 737-400. As can be seen most instruments are replicated, with the large EFIS displays prominent.

BOTTOM LEFT: Overhead cockpit instruments and switches.

BELOW LEFT: This is the cockpit instrumentation of a 737-300 which, like all modern airliners, features EFIS and FMS displays. The large trim wheels in the centre are standard on Boeing aircraft.

ABOVE: The Next Generation 737 features an updated and revised layout for cockpit instrumentation, with three large EFIS displays in a more central position.

RIGHT: Cockpit schematic showing major panel and joystick instrumentation.

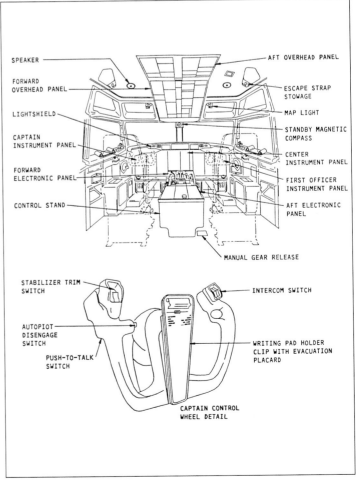

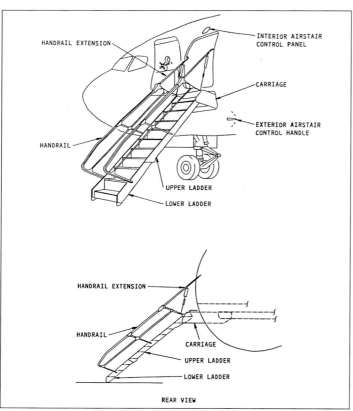

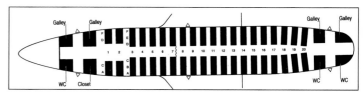

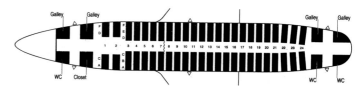

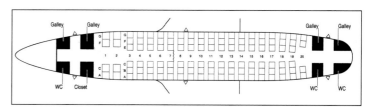

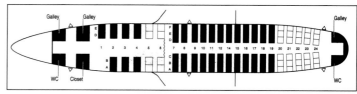

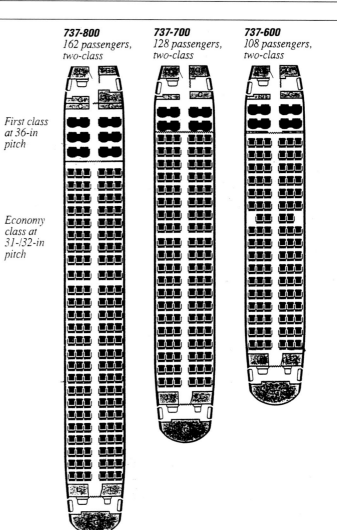

737-800
162 passengers, two-class

737-700
128 passengers, two-class

737-600
108 passengers, two-class

First class at 36-in pitch

Economy class at 31-/32-in pitch

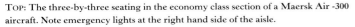

TOP: The three-by-three seating in the economy class section of a Maersk Air -300 aircraft. Note emergency lights at the right hand side of the aisle.

ABOVE: For an aircraft of its size the 737 has spacious overhead storage bins.

ABOVE LEFT: Seating configurations vary considerably. In its 737-400s, for instance, British Airways operates a mixed business/economy cabin with a movable divider. A feature becoming increasingly common among airlines, it allows increased business passengers to be carried — and so increased yield. British Airways also differentiates between Gatwick and Heathrow-based aircraft. Aircraft based at the latter are configured with 141 seats, six fewer than those at its other London base.

The 737-300 and -400 have proved popular with Europe's charter airlines, but configurations vary. British charter operators have configured the -400 with 170 seats whereas German operators operate with fewer — Germans are happy to pay more for their ticket providing they have more leg room. Other differences include galley fits, which for airlines with shorter journey sectors may not feature an oven, serving cold snacks only.

From the top these drawings show: (A) Garuda 737-400 in business/economy fit. but due to the shorter sector lengths this airline omits one galley and WC from the rear of the aircraft; (B) Ansett Australia Airlines 737-300 which, due to longer sector lengths, features additional galley and WC compared to Garuda; (C and D) Qantas features a three-class layout on its 737s, both the -300 and -400.

LEFT: Reproduced from Boeing press releases is this possible seating configurations for the -600/-700/-800. This can range from just 108 passengers in a two-class layout on the -600 to 162 passengers in a similar layout on the larger -800. The latter can, and probably will, carry as many as 189 in all-economy charter configuration.

ABOVE RIGHT: The forward stowage area for catering trolleys.

RIGHT: The forward galley area and service door on the starboard side of a Series -300 aircraft. On the left is a fold-up cabin crew seat.

FAR LEFT: Passenger access is two doors on the port side of the aircraft, the forward having integral stairs on the lower fuselage (TOP LEFT). For access to the galley areas by catering crews, there are co-located doors on the starboard side.

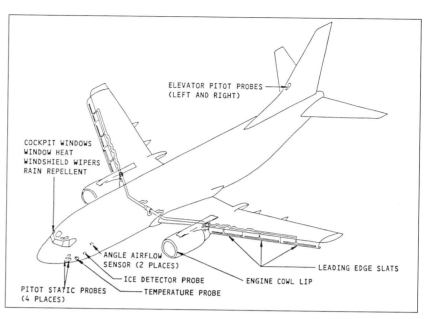

ABOVE: Anti-ice components diagram. Note engine bleed air thermal anti-icing to prevent formation of ice on the wing leading edge slats and engine cowl lip.

LEFT: Underwing refuelling points require only a small ladder for access by refuelling crew, which can be achieved by just one person.

BELOW: The large trailing edge flaps are evident in this shot. Note the rearward facing wingtip light. All 737 variants feature overwing exits which, by law, are outlined by a distinctive colour so they can be easily located from the outside of the aircraft. The higher capacity variants, the -400, -800 and -900 have two overwing exits.

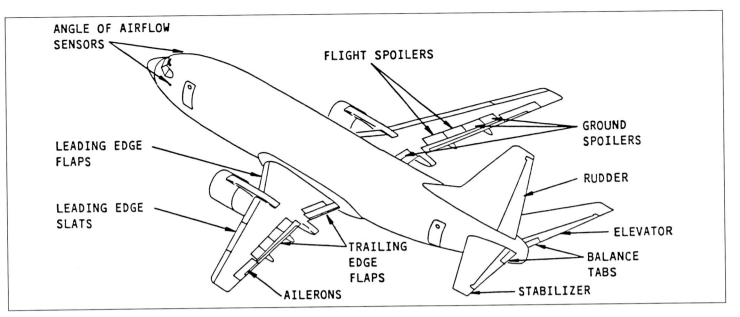

ABOVE: The primary flight controls are the hydraulically operated ailerons, elevators and rudder. there are two hydraulic systems to provide cover should one fail — and even in the unlikely event of both doing so the ailerons and elevators may be handled manually. High lift for take-off is provided by trailing edge flaps and leading edge flaps and slats.

BELOW: 737-300 exterior lighting showing the position and function of all the upper surface lights.

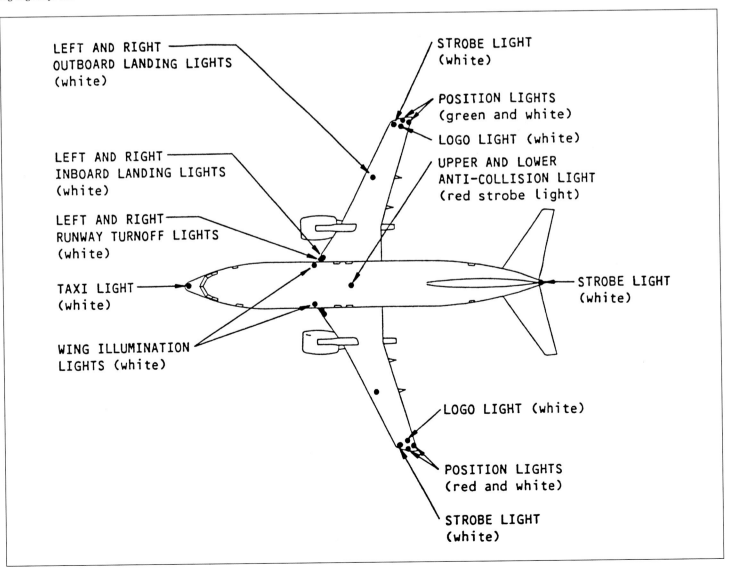

5 IN SERVICE

SERIES -300

The series -300 was the first of the new generation 737s, with the go-ahead coming in March 1981 following orders from Southwest Airlines and USAir for 10 each and options for a further 20 planes. Southwest has since gone on to become the largest -300 operator having recently taken delivery of its 186th and last of the type. Southwest is also the largest 737 operator worldwide, with a total of 258 aircraft, including 47 -200s and 25 -500s, with deliveries of the first of 63 -700s imminent. United Airlines is second in this league table with a fleet of 221 aircraft, though it currently has none at all on order.

Home Customers

The first 737-300 (the 1,001st 737 built) took to the air on 24 February 1984. The second followed within two weeks and was delivered to USAir on 28 November that year, by which time another US carrier, Piedmont, had ordered 15 of the type. As it happened, in 1989 Piedmont was taken over by USAir, and for some time these aircraft were flown in hybrid markings.

For the first couple of years sales of the -300 proved disappointing, though one significant order was that for 10 aircraft from the International Lease Finance Corporation (ILFC), the first of many orders Boeing has received from one of the largest leasing companies in the world.

A number of the US majors operate series -300s — some by default through buy-outs. New York Air was an early customer in 1985, however the company was merged into Continental Airlines in 1987 to whom the aircraft were transferred. The year 1987 also saw Delta Airlines inherit 13 -300s when it took over Western Airlines, and American did likewise with Air Cal, though American has leased the aircraft to other carriers, notably Southwest.

It was a surprise in 1985 when Sunworld International Airways acquired the first of four leased examples, though the airline ceased operations towards the end of 1988. After Southwest, United Airlines has the largest -300 fleet which currently numbers 101, deliveries started back in 1986. Some of these are now flown in 'Shuttle by United' titles — the airline's low cost West Coast operation.

America West now has a substantial fleet of 42 -300s operating alongside a smaller fleet of -200s. In Hawaii, Aloha Airlines' -200s are amongst the hardest working planes anywhere due to the short inter-island sectors. One of the airline's -200s suffered a well publicised failure in 1988 when, due to corrosion, the fuselage roof peeled back in-flight like a sardine can. Fortunately the mortally wounded aircraft managed to land safely with the loss of only one life, but inspection of similar aged aircraft in the fleet prompted the airline to order a pair of -300s as hasty replacements.

South America

In subsequent years the series -300 has been the favoured mount of many of the new 'start-ups' in the US, such as Western Pacific, Vanguard and Frontier, the latter also operating a number of -200s.

In South America, (particularly in Brazil) the -300 has proved popular in operation with major carriers Varig, VASP and TransBrasil. The latter ordered the first of 11 with deliveries commencing in 1986, the other two carriers following suit a year later. Mexican carrier TAESA has two -300s in its predominantly Boeing fleet. Elsewhere on the continent only TACA and, more recently, Lloyd Aero Boliviano seem to have found the resources to acquire the -300 — the many other 737 operators in the continent staying faithful to their ageing -200s. Some, such as Avensa, Aviateca, Ladeco and Pluna have briefly operated leased examples of the -300.

European Operators

Back in 1968 it was quite a surprise when charter company Britannia Airways became the first UK company to operate the 737. It was as much a surprise when another UK charter operator Orion Airways became the first, not just in Europe, but outside the US to select the series -300. Four aircraft were ordered in 1982, and ultimately seven -300 aircraft wore Orion's brown, yellow and white colours before the company ceased operations in 1988 when it was taken over by the Thomson Group. The aircraft were then transferred to Britannia Airways, Thomson's in-house airline.

Within a few years the -300 began to appear in the colours of several other British operators; Dan-Air in 1985, Air Europe and British Midland in 1987, and Inter European and Monarch the following year. Of those mentioned three no longer exist. British Midland still operates a substantial fleet of new genera-

TOP RIGHT: Following close on the heels of Southwest as the biggest user of 737s is United Airlines. This major carrier operates the series -200, -300 and -500. A number of the latter two variants are operated in 'Shuttle by United' markings, the Shuttle being United's low-cost operation based in California aimed to compete with Southwest. Photographed inbound to Los Angeles is 737-322 N394UA.

CENTRE RIGHT: Southwest Airlines has the largest 737 fleet and took delivery of its 186th and final series -300 in the autumn of 1997. Future deliveries will be the new -700. Southwest has a number of aircraft in special colour schemes, including 737-3H4 N609SW *California One* painted in the colours of the California flag, complete with 'grizzly'. The aircraft was photographed at the airline's busiest hub, Phoenix, Arizona.

RIGHT: Photographed in US Air livery at Toronto is 737-3B7 N375US which was delivered to the airline in November 1984 as N354AU. Third in the league table of 737 operators is US Airways, previously known as USAir. The airline unfortunately appears high in the attrition stakes having lost three New Generation 737s.

ABOVE: Although Britannia Airways was the first European operator of the Boeing 737 back in 1968 it never ordered the new generation series of 737. However, due to the demise of Orion Airways, Britannia inherited the -300s operated by that company. These were successfully integrated into Britannia's inventory until disposed of in favour of the 757 and 767. Photographed at Gatwick is former Orion 737-3T5 G-BNRT.

ABOVE RIGHT: Air China is the Chinese national carrier and operates an extensive fleet of Boeing aircraft comprising 737s, 767s and several variants of the 747. The airline has 19 737-300s, a number of which were handed down from CAAC. Illustrated at Beijing's Capital airport is 737-3J6 B-2949. These aircraft are flown in a one-class 140-seat configuration.

tion 737s, while Monarch disposed of its last of the type as recently as April 1997, (the aircraft in question now plying its trade with easyJet). In fact easyJet now operates only the -300, having disposed of the -200s it started operations with in 1995. In 1988 EuroBerlin France was an airline set up jointly by Air France and Lufthansa to operate from Berlin's Tegel airport, but the six aircraft were British registered and operated by Monarch, though the airline ceased operations in 1995. Other British charter operators who have flown the 737-300 briefly include Air Foyle, Air 2000 and Excalibur. The series -300 also appeared in British Airways livery for a short period as four of the variant were leased from Maersk Air for a couple of years prior to the airline taking delivery of its -400s. There are two -300s currently operating in BA livery. These former TransBrasil aircraft were delivered to TAT European Airlines in March 1996 and are used on services to London's Gatwick and Heathrow airports. The airline has just announced it is to lease seven -300s with delivery commencing in December 1997. These aircraft will be operated from Birmingham and Manchester on routes to some European destinations where the noisy -200 is no longer welcome.

In mainland Europe JAT – Yugoslav Airlines took delivery of the first of nine aircraft in 1985, but it was during the next couple of years that the series -300 really began to appear in the colours of many of Europe's major carriers. In 1986 KLM, Lauda Air and Lufthansa were all recipients. Air Europa, the Spanish affiliate of Britain's Air Europe received its first in 1987, and the airline currently operates 12 of this variant. The Norwegian affiliate, Norway Airlines operated two, and in 1989 changed its name to Air Europe Scandinavia, before it too suspended operations due to financial difficulties. Denmark's Maersk Air has, and still operates large numbers of -300s, many of which are leased out to other carriers. The Belgian national airline Sabena and its charter subsidiary Sobelair took delivery of -300s in 1987, as did charter carriers Germania and

Hispania. The latter has since ceased operations but the former continues to go from strength to strength and is currently operating 13 aircraft.

In Germany Hapag-Lloyd briefly operated the -300 alongside other variants, Condor still does so, while Deutsche BA currently utilises 12 of the type with a further seven on order. Aer Lingus took two -300s in 1987, but these have since been disposed of as the airline concentrates on the series -400 and -500s. The Portuguese national carrier TAP currently has 10 -300s, though charter airlines Air Atlantis and Air Columbus have both ceased operations, passing on their -300s to others. One other Portuguese operator is SATA – Air Acores which took delivery of a leased -300 in October 1995 to link the Azores Islands with Lisbon. Staying in the Iberian Peninsula, Viva Air was formed in 1988 as an Iberia subsidiary to operate charter and low yield scheduled services bringing holidaymakers to Spain. It no longer operates scheduled services for its parent company, but its fleet of nine -300s are kept busy on charter work. Universair was a new Spanish charter airline founded in 1987 with orders for two -300s, though its existence was brief.

In neighbouring France, Aeromaritime was a charter subsidiary of UTA, however when that company was taken over by Air France in 1991 the fleet of six -300s were transferred to the new owner. Corse Air operated a pair of -300s from Ajaccio,

this airline no longer exists, but similar sounding Corsair, a charter carrier, still does though it has disposed of its -300s in favour of the larger -400. The largest -300 operator in France is L'Aeropostale with a fleet of 15 QC (Quick Change) aircraft. As the nomenclature suggests the aircraft are used on night postal operations, but are also used for passenger work during the daytime, often on Air France flights. In Amsterdam, Transavia Airlines was formed by KLM back in 1965 to operate charter flights, but the airline has expanded considerably and also operates some scheduled services with a fleet of 737s, 12 of which are -300s. Also based at Amsterdam is Air Holland; formed in 1985 it currently operates three -300s on European charter routes.

Air Belgium took delivery of a leased -300 in 1987 and this aircraft is still operated alongside a -400. Brussels based Trans European Airways (TEA) was formed in 1970 to operate charter services, initially with Boeing 720, 707 and then Airbus A300 equipment, before eventually choosing the 737-300. In a similar fashion to Air Europe, it then set up subsidiary companies such as TEA Basel, TEA France, TEA Italy and TEA UK in other European countries in the period 1988-90. Apart from TEA Basel, all had identical liveries which helped as aircraft were often moved from one operator to another to meet short term demands. In 1991 however the parent company suffered financial problems and TEA operations ceased. However TEA Basel managed to remain operational, and soon afterwards changed the name to TEA Switzerland. It currently operates five -300s, and in 1993 formed a subsidiary, TEA Cyprus. The airline of another Mediterranean island, Air Malta operates -300s alongside its older -200s, all three aircraft being delivered in the spring of 1993.

The TEA livery made a reappearance in the skies of Europe when Euro Belgian Airlines (EBA) was formed from the ashes of TEA. This time the airline was very successful, and at one time its fleet numbers reached double figures, predominantly

-300s, but also -400s. However in 1996 its colours once more disappeared, as the airline changed name as a result of a joint venture with Richard Branson's empire, thus Virgin Express was born. Still Brussels based, the newcomer operates a number of scheduled services, some on behalf of Sabena, as well as charter work at weekends.

Meanwhile in Italy, Air One has recently commenced domestic services in competition with Alitalia, for which it uses six leased -300s, the first of these was taken on charge in 1995. Another newcomer over the Mediterranean is Cronus Airlines. Formed in 1995 with a single 737-300 the Athens based company has just added a second plane to its fleet for holiday charters.

Over the past decade Turkey has been renowned for the number of short-lived charter airlines which seem to exist for a year or two before disappearing. In this category fall Birgenair, Bosphorus Airways and Sultan Air, all of which at one time have operated the -300. Sun Express Airlines was formed in 1990 by Lufthansa to operate charter flights between Germany and Turkey, equipped with new 737-300s, three of which are currently in use.

The Former Soviet Bloc

Without doubt one of the most difficult areas for Boeing's marketing team to penetrate was the Soviet bloc nations of Eastern Europe. Finding funds to purchase or lease modern Western equipment for most of these carriers would be extremely difficult, having been used to operating Soviet types such as the Tu-134, Tu-154 and Yak-42 which they would have acquired at low cost. Boeing's first ex-Iron Curtain success was with Hungary's Malev Airlines who took delivery of four -300s in 1991. One surprise however was the decision of Turkmenistan Airlines to take a 737-300. This was delivered in November 1992, and followed by two more in August 1994. Air Ukraine International was formed in 1992, its sole equipment being

737s acquired to serve a number of Europe's capitals from Kiev. The airline has operated the -200, -300 and -400, all on lease. Only the former is operated at present, though a -300 is currently on order. To avoid confusion with the much larger Air Ukraine, (whose livery is confusingly very similar) the airline has since changed its name to Ukraine International Airlines. Tarom of Romania has a fleet of five -300s which were delivered from 1993 onwards, whilst LOT has recently added three -300s to supplement its fleet of -400 and -500s for the summer of 1997.

In 1996 a new airline, Fischer Air was formed in the Czech Republic to operate charters to the Mediterranean holiday resorts, and the airline's two brand new -300s were delivered just in time for the 1997 summer season.

The Far East

Despite success elsewhere, the Asian market proved to be a difficult nut to crack for Boeing's sales teams. Although Pakistan International Airlines was an early customer with an order for six aircraft in 1985, it was four more years before any more orders for this variant were forthcoming from the region. These were from Garuda and Philippines Airlines. In 1994 a new Malaysian carrier, Air Asia, was formed and operates a pair of series -300s out of Kuala Lumpur with a further example on order.

Malaysia Airlines has a large fleet of 737-400s, but it also utilises a pair of -300 freighters in its MASKargo division. In the neighbouring island of Singapore the national airline used to operate a single 737-300 freighter on regional cargo services, though the aircraft has now been disposed of. However Singapore Airlines has a subsidiary named SilkAir which operates regional services using a fleet of six 737-300s, (though the airline has recently selected Airbus products to replace its Boeings). In nearby former war-torn Vietnam, Hang Khong

Vietnam, which became Vietnam Airlines used 737-300s operated by TEA Switzerland on its route network, prior to adopting the Airbus A320 for regional services.

Having made inroads into the Chinese market it was perhaps inevitable that it would only be a matter of time before the -300 would be seen in Chinese skies. The Civil Aviation Administration of China (CAAC) already operated the -200, and eight -300s were ordered to complement them. These aircraft however were not in CAAC livery for very long as the Chinese authorities decided the CAAC should operate strictly as the regulatory body. Hence a number of new airlines were formed to take over the running of the various regional divisions of CAAC, these adopted appropriate names such as China Eastern, China Northern, China Southern etc. The first two mentioned have sizeable fleets of McDonnell-Douglas and Airbus products, however China Southern with a fleet of 23 -300s and 11 -500s is the largest 737 operator in the country.

The series -300 has proved to be an extremely popular aircraft in China, and almost 120 of the variant are operated by a number of carriers. These include; Air China, China National Aviation Corporation, China Southern, China Southwest, China United, China Xinhua, China Xinjiang, China Yunnan, Hainan Airlines, Shandong Airlines, Shanghai Airlines, Shenzhen Airlines, Wuhan Airlines, Xiamen Airlines and Zhongyuan Airlines.

Australasia and the Pacific

In Australia Ansett Airlines ordered a batch of 16 737s, most were delivered in 1986, with the first aircraft being named *Waltzing Mathilda*. Competitor Trans Australian Airways also ordered 16 planes, the delivery of which coincided with a name change to Australian Airlines. As it happens the company has since been acquired by state carrier Qantas in whose colours they now operate. The sole -300 operator in New Zealand is

Freedom Air International, a subsidiary of the Mount Cook Line founded in 1995 principally to operate Trans-Tasman charters to Australia. This was to combat the success of new-born low cost operator Kiwi Travel International operating similar flights from its base at Hamilton, initially with a Boeing 727, and later a 737-400. Mount Cook is in fact a subsidiary of Air New Zealand, and the ploy of forming Freedom Air has obviously worked as Kiwi Travel International has recently suspended operations.

In the nearby South Pacific area, airlines from a number of the small island nations have found the 737-300 an ideal aircraft for their route structure. These are AirCalin, (formerly Air Caledonie International) Air Pacific, Polynesian Airlines, Royal Tongan and Solomons Airlines, all of whom operate single examples.

Africa

The African continent is home to less than 10 series -300s. Air Madagascar and Air Malawi both have single examples while Kenya Airways has just taken delivery of two new -300s in March and May 1997 in place of the -200s previously employed. Cameroon Airlines has just added a leased example to its fleet. Off the coast of Madagascar is the tiny island of

BELOW LEFT: Alaska International Air changed its name to Markair in 1984 to coincide with the delivery of five Boeing 737-200s. The Anchorage based carrier later added the series -300 and -400 to its inventory, however due to financial difficulties the airline ceased operations in 1995. Illustrated about to land at Los Angeles is series -400 N686MA.

BELOW: European launch customer for the 737-400 was newly formed charter operator Air UK Leisure. The first of five planned was delivered in October 1988, and ultimately the airline had seven on charge. Featured is the second aircraft, G-UKLB *Flagship St. Bernard.* The airline has since changed its name to Leisure International Airways and currently operates Airbus A320s, A321 and Boeing 767 equipment.

Reunion where Air Austral has a single -300 with another slated to join it.

Military Usage

To date there have only been three military customers for -300 series, two of whom are from Asia. The Republic of Korea Air Force has a single example used as a government/VIP aircraft. The Royal Flight of the Royal Thai Air Force also had a -300, until it was lost in an accident. (See Chapter 8). The other customer is the Mexican Air Force who acquired the aircraft secondhand in January 1992.

SERIES -400

Piedmont Airlines was obviously pleased with the series -300 as, in June 1986 the airline became the launch customer for the -400 with an order for 25 with options for a further 30. The first aircraft was delivered on 15 September 1988, not long after USAir had announced its order for 50 737s. The first 20 were for the -300, but the airline kept its options open for the remainder, and ultimately chose the -400 to fill some of the places. In August the following year USAir took over Piedmont and inherited its substantial fleet of 737s which, at the time, included 19 -400s, making it the world's leading 737 operator. USAir ultimately had around 240 737s in its inventory — though it has now dropped to third position behind Southwest and United due to the recent disposal of several -200s as it struggles to reduce costs. Towards the end of 1996 the airline announced a new image, introducing a new livery and name-change to US Airways.

Despite the popularity of the series -300 in the US, home based airlines have been slow to adapt to the -400. It was 1992 before the next US operators — both with strong Alaskan connections — joined the club. Anchorage based Markair took delivery of the first of five in March 1992, while Alaska Airlines

which, despite the name, is based at Seattle, Washington received its first a month later. Unfortunately Markair ceased operations in 1995. Alaska Airlines meanwhile continues to flourish, and now has 25 in use with a further 12 to be delivered over the next couple of years.

Later in 1992 Fort Lauderdale based Carnival Airlines received its first 737-400, and now has seven in use. As Aloha Airlines strived to update its fleet it took delivery of a pair too, and although these machines have since been disposed of, the company plans to replace them some time in the future. The only other current US operator of the -400 is Pro Air. Launched in late 1996 the airline took delivery in April 1997 of a pair of new aircraft to be operated on charters from Detroit.

Conquering Europe

As Lufthansa had operated all three 737 variants to date, naturally Boeing had strong hopes that the German carrier would be its European launch customer for the -400. It is true the airline had a requirement for such an aircraft, however its needs were pressing and as it was looking exceedingly unlikely that the Boeing product would be ready by 1988 the company looked elsewhere. Airbus and its new A320 however would be ready in time and the Germans opted for the European product. Lufthansa eventually did join the -400 club, with all 11 delivered in just four months in 1992. Strangely though the -400 seemed a misfit in the airline's inventory, and a few were soon leased out to other operators. As these words are written Lufthansa has just sold its last few -400s and the type is no longer on the inventory.

The European launch customer proved to be a surprise. Like the -300 it turned out to be a newly launched British char-

ter airline, this time Air UK Leisure. The airline's first plane was the third -400 built and was delivered in October 1988. The airline ultimately operated seven of the type, all of which have recently been transferred to KLM, some via lease to Modiluft in India. Another UK charter operator was Novair, which took delivery of a pair in the spring of 1989, but the airline ceased operations in May the following year. Air Europe and Inter European Airways also operated the -400 for a short time alongside the -300s before they too ceased operations.

The ability of the -400 to carry up to 170 passengers in charter configuration proved a strong attraction to a number of Europe's charter airlines, particularly as it had the range to operate non-stop from Western Europe to the Canary Islands and the eastern Mediterranean. Air Berlin currently operates nine, the first being delivered in April 1990, and the latest in May 1997. Hapag-Lloyd took delivery of four in 1989, and its -400 fleet has since grown to 12 aircraft.

Other European charter airlines have also found the -400 to be an ideal type. In Spain, Air Europa has five with another on order, the type joining the inventory in April 1994, while Futura's fleet is ever expanding and now numbers 11. Nortjet also operated three 1400s during its brief two year existence. Air Belgium has a single example, Sobelair three, while Corsair has had a pair since 1992. A new French operator is Star Europe which utilises the former Aloha pair alongside a -300 and two new A320s.

Pegasus was Turkey's first -400 operator in April 1990, the fleet currently comprising five machines. Istanbul Airlines which started as a charter carrier in 1989, now also offers scheduled services with six aircraft, and Sun Express supplements its -300 fleet with a pair of leased -400s. Nordic European Airlines, (formerly Nordic East) has a single -400, though at the time of writing it is on short term lease to Deutsche BA. Another Nordic carrier is Maersk Air, but it has disposed of its -400s which used to operate on the carrier's charter network. During the winter of 1996-97 Egypt's AMC Aviation utilised a single -400 on lease from Futura.

BELOW: It was a sad day for British aviation when Dan-Air succumbed to financial difficulties in 1992 and, even sadder when, like British Caledonian before it, it was subsumed into British Airways. For the second time a British Conservative government stood by as domestic and, to a lesser extent, international competition to B.A. was removed at a stroke. Dan-Air's fleet of leased 737-400s was acquired by B.A., and for a time operated in the hybrid marks displayed on G-BVNM. Note the thrust reverser deployed.

It wasn't just Europe's charter airlines who decided the -400 was the ideal aircraft for their routes and, unlike their US counterparts, many of Europe's major scheduled carriers rushed to order the latest model from Renton. British Midland added the type to the 737-300s which recently joined the company. Two were delivered initially, though one was soon the result of a highly publicised accident at Kegworth. (See Chapter 7.) Over the years the airline has steadily built up its 737 fleet and it currently has six -400s. Also in 1988 Dan-Air added a pair of -400s to join a newly acquired -300, and by the time the airline was taken over by British Airways it had a 12 strong -400 fleet. In 1989 there was a rush of activity as 737-400s joined the fleets of Aer Lingus, Braathens, Icelandair and KLM.

Icelandair received the first four in April, and Braathens its first in June. The Norwegian carrier uses the type on both scheduled and charter work, with the seventh and last aircraft delivered in March 1997. Aer Lingus received the first of six in July 1989, while KLM welcomed the first of the type in September. The KLM fleet has steadily grown to 19 aircraft including the recently acquired former Air UK Leisure machines.

The year 1990 was a quiet one for the -400 in Europe, with Royal Air Maroc taking two, though the airline has since increased this number to seven. Another flurry of activity followed in 1991 as numerous 737-400s made their delivery flight eastbound across the Atlantic. Turk Hava Yollari received the first of a large order for 28 aircraft in February, with deliveries being completed by May 1993. To supplement its ageing -200 fleet, Olympic Airways had taken delivery of six in just three months, with a seventh following two years later. In Austria Lauda Air received two, while Belgium's Sabena received the first of three aircraft, in both cases supplementing -300s received earlier.

Probably the most important order of all — in Boeing's eyes at least — was that for 24 aircraft for British Airways, though to Europeans it came as no surprise as many say the letters BA stand for 'Boeing Always'! The first aircraft of this order (G-DOCA) was the 1,000th new generation 737 built, and was delivered to the airline in October 1991. Most of the Europe-bound aircraft in 1992 were destined to fill the BA and THY orders, though two were delivered to Luxair early in the year.

The first -400s delivered to Eastern Europe was a pair on lease from Guinness-Peat to Air Ukraine International in November 1992, though two years later they joined the growing 737 fleet at Malev. In the intervening period LOT received its first in April 1993, with a further six following over the next four years. In the first quarter of 1995 CSA leased a pair from Malaysia Airlines. These are still in use with three new aircraft on order for 1998 delivery. Gatwick based GB Airways, (formerly known as Gibair) is now a British Airways franchise carrier and operates its aircraft in BA livery on a number of routes principally to the Iberian Peninsula and North Africa. In March 1995 two of the former Dan-Air -400s acquired by BA were transferred to GB Airways, and the airline now has five -400s on strength.

As previously mentioned under the series -300, Euro Belgian Airlines became Virgin Express in 1996, and the airline's fleet includes a number of series -400s. The latest -400 news from Europe is the April 1997 announcement by Aeroflot of an order of 10 aircraft with one due per month from April 1998.

India

Some deregulation in the Indian market has seen a number of new entrants in the 1990s. Modiluft was formed with assistance from Lufthansa who supplied some -200s on lease, while Air UK Leisure supplied three -400s on lease in October 1995. Both European carriers however, claimed that lease payments

BELOW: Malaysia Airlines is easily the largest Asian operator of the -400. At the time of its order Malaysian had a fleet of around a dozen -200s, and it was quite a surprise when the airline announced an order for twenty -400s with options on many more. The first was delivered in April 1992, and forty-two -400s have been delivered, though some of these are leased to other carriers in the region. Photographed on a visit to Bangkok is 737-4H6 9M-MQI

were not forthcoming and took court action to solve the problem. The outcome is that Modiluft has currently ceased operations, while claiming they are the innocent party. Jet Airways is however, still in operation. This carrier commenced operations in 1992 and operates a sizeable fleet of new generation 737s, seven of which are leased -400s with a further four new examples on order from Boeing. Also formed in 1992, Sahara India Airlines fleet is much smaller, two -400s being leased from ILFC in October 1994.

Success in the Far East

The series -400 has without doubt been extremely successful in Europe, and this success is mirrored in Asia. In South Korea Asiana Airlines was formed in December 1988 and quickly took delivery of new series -400s; 19 are now in use with a further two on order. Thai Airways International selected the 737-400, the first of which was delivered to Bangkok in August 1990. The airline received a further four in August 1997 taking its total to 11.

One of the largest orders ever from an Asian carrier was that by Malaysia Airlines for 27 new generation 737s. This included 20 -400s, though that number was increased and eventually accounted for some 42 aircraft, deliveries spanned five years from April 1992. A number of these have been leased out to other carriers, particularly emerging Asian ones. These include a pair to Myanmar Airways International in August 1994, and a pair to Royal Air Cambodge. The latter carrier ceased operations in mid-1997 and the aircraft returned to Malaysian. Garuda Indonesian was the recipient of seven aircraft in the final quarter of 1993.

Despite the mass air travel in Japan Boeing failed to make inroads into the domestic market with the 737. The exception was South West Airlines based in Okinawa with series -200s. The airline is now known as Japan Transocean Air and is affiliated to Japan Airlines. The first of three -400s was delivered in June 1994 with a further four to follow. Japan Airlines itself recently joined the 737 club with the first of eight -400s delivered in May 1995, with deliveries completed by March 1998.

While there are well over 100 series -300 operating in China the number of -400s does not reach double figures. It was as recently as July 1995 that the first of this variant was imported, thanks to Hainan Airlines who received four. China Xinhua received its sole -400 in March 1996. In each case these aircraft operate alongside series -300s. In neighbouring Taiwan, China Airlines received six -400s in November and December of 1996, finally allowing the airline to dispose of its ageing -200s.

Australasia and the Pacific

Down under, Australian Airlines ordered a batch of 16 aircraft which were delivered during 1989-90. Due to the takeover by Qantas these machines now operate in the livery of the national carrier, and the number of aircraft has been increased to 22. Air Vanuatu began operating a leased Australian Airlines -400 in 1992, and the agreement now continues with Qantas.

Air Nauru is the airline named for its tiny Pacific island home. It has operated 737s for many years, and its inventory presently comprises a single -400 acquired in August 1993. Solomons Airlines operated a -400 from 1992 to 1994, however this aircraft has subsequently been replaced by a series -300.

South America

In South America only TransBrasil currently operates the 737-400, and it received the first three leased examples in 1989.

Military Uptake

The sole military customer for the -400 is the Royal Thai Air Force who have used it in the VIP role since it was delivered in February 1995.

SERIES -500

The series -500 was the logical successor for those airlines with ageing -200s in their inventory. Norway's Braathens and Southwest Airlines in the US were launch customers for the -500, with orders for 25 and 20 respectively, though Southwest also took options on a further 20.

Southwest was the first recipient of a -500 in February 1990,

ABOVE: Like Hapag-Lloyd, the colours on Denmark's Maersk Air fleet are perhaps better known on the company's large fleet of ocean going ships. The airline was founded in 1969 to operate charters throughout Europe's major holiday spots. Although the company still employs aircraft in this role it is steadily increasing its scheduled work. Fokker 50s are used internally, while Boeing 737s are used on services to other Scandinavian countries as well as to London/Gatwick, with a new Copenhagen-Geneva service planned. Displaying the airline's pleasing blue livery at Gatwick is 737-5L9 OY-APC. This aircraft was delivered in October 1996 and is the fourth of a batch of eleven new aircraft.

LEFT: Lufthansa has not yet ordered the Next Generation 737 - and is unlikely to do so as its Airbus fleet is adequate for its needs. The airline has however operated all earlier variants from the -100 through to the -500. Illustrated on approach to Heathrow in the airline's current livery is 737-530 D-ABIX named after the town of 'Iserlohn'.

however it eventually cancelled 15 options for the variant. Braathens took delivery of its first machine a month later, and only recently completed the order with the delivery of the 24th of the type. In the US sales could perhaps be viewed as disappointing, with United and Continental being the only other operators. The former took delivery of 57 aircraft between November 1990 and August 1993, but it was February 1994 before Continental took delivery of its first -500. A total of 67 are destined for the airline with deliveries scheduled continuing through to 1999.

European Uptake

The situation in Europe however, couldn't have been more different as many of the continent's major carriers now operate the series -500. Following on the heels of Braathens came fellow Scandinavians Maersk Air and Linjeflyg. The former has just taken delivery of a new batch of five, while five delivered in 1990 are leased to Asiana and Maersk Air UK — the latter being a British Airways franchise carrier operating in the UK carriers livery.

Linjeflyg's aircraft are also now UK based. The airline was taken over by SAS in January 1993, but after only a short period in that carrier's markings the aircraft were progressively transferred to British Midland. In May 1990 Hapag-Lloyd received the first of five, with Aer Lingus taking the first of its

10 in October. Lufthansa has 30 of the variant, all being delivered inside a year beginning December 1990. The same month Balkan Bulgarian received two of three on order; the first East European airline to operate the variant.

The following year (1991) Air France received its first machines, and fellow French carriers Air Charter, Europe Aero Service and Euralair all eventually joined the -500 club. Belgium's Sabena completed a 'new generation' set when the first of six -500s was delivered in May 1991. In 1992 a further two East European carriers, namely CSA Czechoslovak Airlines and LOT Polish Airlines had their first machines delivered. In June 1992 THY Turkish Airlines received the first of two to complement its growing fleet of -400s. Luxair received two in 1993 with a further pair following in 1995.

After the initial rush of orders from European airlines there was a period of quiet on the western front until Estonian Air took delivery of a -500 in June 1995 with a second following in February 1996. These were the first western built airliners to be operated in the newly independent country.

Africa

In North Africa three national carriers operate the series -500; Egyptair, Royal Air Maroc and Tunis Air. The latter received the first of four in April 1992, with the other airlines being recipients the previous year. Egyptair has also just leased one of its aircraft to Air Sinai, replacing a series -200.

Success in Asia

For the number of customers, if not the number of aircraft, Asia has been a successful area for Boeing's salesmen. Korea's fledgling Asiana Airlines received its first in August 1990 and currently has six in use, including one on lease from Maersk Air. In China, China Southern Airlines fleet of -500s currently numbers 11, the first being delivered in 1991. Despite the success of the 737 in China the only other -500 operators are Xiamen Airlines with seven aircraft, four of which are leased from Braathens, though one example has since been sub-leased to Fujian Airlines.

Meanwhile, in July 1992 the Malaysian national carrier began to take delivery of nine series -500 alongside its ever expanding inventory of the larger -400. Air Nippon is Japan's sole operator of the type with deliveries currently in progress. Towards the end of 1997 Garuda started to receive the first of five on order.

The Rest of the World
Jet Airways in India operates a single example of the type alongside its -300s and -400s, while Fiji's Air Pacific also has a single example of the type which was delivered in 1992.

Rio Sul Airlines is the only current -500 operator in South America, having received the first of its 10 brand new aircraft in 1992, with a further two presently on order. Fellow Brazilian carrier Nordeste briefly operated one on lease, but has recently placed an order for two. Similar sounding Mexican operator Noroeste as well as Taesa no longer operate this variant.

The only African airline operating the -500 is Uganda Airlines which received its single aircraft in July 1995.

Military -500s
There are just two military operators, both in South America. The Peruvian Air Force operates one aircraft delivered in September 1995 on government VIP duties, and the Chilean Air Force followed suite in September 1997.

SERIES -600
Of the Next Generation series 737s the series -600 has the least orders to date. Launch customer is SAS Scandinavian Airlines which announced an order for 35 aircraft in March 1995. This was later increased to total 41 aircraft, with first deliveries due in mid-1998. This was perhaps a surprise order on two counts. Firstly, the airline has been a loyal McDonnell-Douglas customer and has a large fleet of DC-9s and MD-80s, and the manufacturer had strong hopes SAS would be the launch customer for the MD-95.

Secondly, although SAS inherited 737-500s from Linjeflyg, the type lasted only a few years in SAS service before being transferred to British Midland. In 1997 Continental Airlines announced an order for 30 -600s.

The major leasing company ILFC ordered 40 of the variant, followed in September 1997 with a repeat order for a further 31. Irish lessor Sunrock Aircraft Corporation announced an order for five at the 1997 Paris Air Show. On 28 October 1997 Tunisair announced an order for four -600s, with options on a further three Next Generation aircraft. The carrier already operates the series -200 and -500.

SERIES -700
While orders for the -600 have been slow to accumulate this certainly has not been the case for the series -700. Delivery of the first of 63 aircraft to launch customer Southwest Airlines took place on 19 December 1997. By the end of 1997 Maersk Air received the first of the six ordered back in June 1994. In December 1994 two German companies had signed orders for the -700. Germania for 12 aircraft to replace its current -300s,

and Bavaria Fluggesellschaft with an order for two plus two options which they have since taken up. Although Bavaria used to be a charter airline it has recently been set up as a leasing company, and two of the aircraft are destined for Russian independent operator Transaero.

Well known lessor ILFC has 11 of the type on order. Elsewhere in Europe TEA Switzerland has two examples on order, whilst in February 1997 Braathens announced an order for six with 10 options, (six of which have since been exercised for delivery between 1998 and the year 2000). Continental is due to take 26 examples as part of its order for all three Next Generation variants. Eastwind Airlines, a small New Jersey based operator ordered two series -700s in October 1997 to replace the pair of elderly -200s currently utilised. A few weeks later Alaska Airlines announced an order for three -700s.

The first South American operator will be independent Argentinean carrier LAPA who, in September 1997, signed a 12 year deal with ILFC for two aircraft.

At the other end of the globe Shanghai Airlines is the sole Asian customer to date with an order for three, with a similar number due to Fiji's Air Pacific. At the moment the latter order is in doubt as the island nation is the recipient of a substantial amount of aid from the European Union, who are not particularly happy that their money is helping to purchase a US product when the Airbus A320 family of aircraft is available. Such practices are not new, and the Americans have employed similar tactics a number of times over the past few decades — notably when Middle East Airlines were alleged to have wanted to buy the VC-10, but were 'obliged' to take the Boeing 707.

Military Orders
In September 1997 Boeing announced the first military order for the Next Generation 737, and what a significant order it could turn out to be. It is for two -700s in QC (Quick Change) configuration for the US Navy. These will replace Douglas C-9B Skytrain II (DC-9) transport aircraft, and are likely to lead to a repeat order for a further 20 or so.

Business Jets
By September 1997 Boeing had taken orders for 25 Boeing Business Jets (BBJ), including one from the golfer Greg Norman and two for engine manufacturer General Electric. Geneva based executive operator Privatair has also signed-up for a pair of Business Jets. On 30 October 1997, during a visit by the Chinese president to the US, an order from China Aviation Supplies for 22 -700s was announced.

SERIES -800
The series -800 has proved to be the most popular of the Next Generation variants with orders from 23 customers to date. German charter airlines Hapag-Lloyd and Air Berlin set the ball rolling in November and December 1994 with orders for 16 and six respectively, and both received their first machines in the first quarter of 1998.

It is the Europeans who have proved most enthusiastic about the -800, particularly those companies whose operations

include long range intra-European charter sectors. Operators such as Euro Belgian Airlines ordered two, and these are likely to be delivered to Virgin Express who now operate the Belgian carrier's services, though the airline may opt to substitute -300s or -400s for fleet commonalty. Lauda Air and LOT also have two on order, while Transavia has eight and Air Europa 10.

During 1997 KLM placed an order for four aircraft for delivery mid-1999 delivery, as did Olympic Airways. Sabre Airways became the first UK customer for a Next Generation 737 with an order for four aircraft for 1998 delivery, presumably to replace the carrier's elderly and noisy Boeing 727s. Due to the increasing European sensitivity over noise issues Denmark's Sterling European Airlines needs to replace its 727s, and in July 1997 announced it had signed a lease agreement for three -800s with another on option. It is likely these aircraft will be from those ordered by ILFC.

In Asia, China Airlines has six examples on order, as has India's Jet Airways who are due to receive the first few aircraft in 1998. Royal Air Maroc with nine on order is the sole customer from the African continent.

Slower US Support

Orders from US carriers have been extremely slow to say the least. It took until November 1996 before the first order was registered, but what a significant order it was! This was American Airlines stunning announcement of a massive order for several Boeing types, with 103 ordered and 'purchase rights' for a further 527 aircraft. This order included 75 737-800s for delivery between 1998 and 2001, however the order was dependent on the successful renegotiation of working practices between the airline and the Allied Pilots Association.

Agreement was eventually agreed between the two parties, however the negotiations became so protracted that the airline lost a number of its early positions on the production line, and it is likely to be 1999 before the first aircraft appears in American Airlines livery. This substantial order also proved controversial in that the airline and the manufacturer agreed that Boeing would be the sole supplier to the airline in the foreseeable future. Similar agreements have since been signed with Delta and Continental Airlines. Delta's order is for 70 Next Generation aircraft, and although the variants and numbers involved were not released at the time of the order, it has since been revealed that all will be for the -800. Continental's initial order was for 30 -800s but this has since been revised down to 22, complementing its orders for the other two variants.

Needless to say the Europeans and Airbus were far from happy over such exclusive agreements, and the European Union threatened sanctions. It was late July 1997 before the EU backed down after the wording of the agreements between Boeing and the three US carriers concerned was changed, whereby it is no longer written down that they will not buy aircraft from another manufacturer. Although the wording has been changed I really don't think it will make any difference, and I think it will be some considerable time before the airlines concerned order an aircraft from Airbus.

To date 51 -800s have been delivered, and 459 ordered — more than any other New Generation aircraft. An early order announced in September 1997 was for one aircraft each for North American Airlines (for delivery in May 1998) and Pegasus Airlines. The latter is a Turkish charter operator which already operates the -400. The following month the Turkish national airline Turk Hava Yollari announced an impressive order for 26 -800s with options on a further 23. Deliveries will be spread over four years from 1998 and replace the -400s they currently use.

SERIES -900

Although Boeing had mooted the variant before, it was still a surprise when on 10 November 1997 the manufacturer announced the launch of the -900 series. Launch customer is Alaskan Airlines with an order for ten aircraft.

6 AIRLINE OPERATORS

A few words of explanation regarding the lists on the following pages:

CAPITAL LETTERS: If the airline name appears in capital letters then that airline is a current 737 operator; if there is no figure for the variants listed then it will be a current operator of another series.

+ The numbers following the plus sign indicate those on order.

* Indicates that an airline once operated that type.

Upper and Lower Case: Those airlines in upper and lower case within brackets indicate that either the airline no longer exists, or that it no longer operates any 737 variant.

Not listed are the many leasing companies which order aircraft direct from Boeing then lease them to the customer airline. It is inevitable that the list below will become out of date very quickly, however the information listed is believed to be accurate as of the end of 1998.

Airline	-300	-400	-500
AB A/L	2	–	–
AER LINGUS	*	6	9
AEROFLOT	–	2 + 8	–
(Aeromaritime)	*	*	–
(Air Afrique)	4	–	–
(Air Aruba)	*	–	–
AIR ASIA	2 + 1	–	–
AIR ATLANTA1	–	–	
(Air Atlantis)	*	–	–
AIR AUSTRAL	2	–	1
AIR BELGIUM	1	1	–
AIR BERLIN	*	9	–
AIRCALIN	1 + 1	–	–
(Air Caledonie Int'l)	*	–	–
(Air California)	*	–	–
AIR CHARTER	*	*	*
AIR CHINA	19	–	–
(Air Columbus)	*	–	–
AIR EUROPA	12	7	–
(Air Europe)	*	*	–

Airline	-300	-400	-500
(Air Foyle)	*	–	–
AIR FRANCE	6	–	18
(Air Guadeloupe)	*	–	–
AIR HOLLAND	3	–	–
AIR MADAGASCAR	1	–	–
AIR MALAWI	1	–	–
AIR MALTA	5	*	–
AIR NAURU	–	1	–
AIR NIPPON	*	–	12 + 2
AIR ONE	6	4	–
AIR PACIFIC	1	–	1
AIR PROVENCE	2	*	–
(Air Reunion)	*	–	–
AIR SINAI	–	–	1
AIR TANZANIA	1	–	–
AIR TROIKA	1	–	–
(Air UK Leisure)	–	*	–
(Air Ukraine Int)	*	*	–
AIR VANUATU	–	1	–
(Air 2000)	*	–	–
ALASKA A/L	–	40	–
ALOHA A/L	*	* + 2	–
AMC	–	1	–
AIR MAINTENANCE Co.			
AMERICA WEST	44	–	–
AMERICAN A/L	*	–	–
AMWAY Corp.	1	–	–
ANGEL AIR	–	–	2
ANSETT AUST	22	–	–

Airline	-300	-400	-500	Airline	-300	-400	-500
AOM	–	–	3	COLOR AIR	2 + 1	–	–
ASIANA	–	19 + 1	1	CSA – CZECH A/L	–	4 + 1	10
(Australian A/L)	*	*	–	(Conair)	*	–	–
AVENSA	*	–	–	CONDOR	2	–	–
AVIATECA	*	–	–	(Constellation Int'l A/L)	*	–	–
BALKAN BULGAR	*	–	3	CONTINENTAL A/L	65	–	64 + 3
(Berlin European)	*	–	–	CORSAIR	*	2	–
(Birgenair)	*	–	–	(Corse Air)	*	–	–
BLUE PANORAMA	–	0 + 2	–	(Country Heights)	*	–	–
(Bosphorus Awys)	*	–	–	CRONUS A/L	2 + 1	1	–
BRAATHENS	–	7	24	(Dan–Air)	*	*	–
(Braniff)	*	–	–	DEBONAIR	1	–	–
(Britannia Awys)	*	–	–	DELTA A/L	15 + 8	–	–
BRITISH AWYS	7	34	–	DEUTSCHE BA	20	*	–
BRITISH MIDLAND	9	5	13	(DFD)	*	–	–
(Cambodia A/L Int'l)	*	–	–	(Duke Farms Inc)	*	–	–
CAMEROON A/L	1	–	–	EASYJET	9 + 9	–	–
(Canair Cargo)	*	–	–	EASYJET SWITZERLAND	5 + 5	–	–
CANARIAS AIR	1	–	–	EGYPTAIR	–	–	4
CARNIVAL A/L	–	7	–	(Emirates)	*	–	–
CAYMAN AWYS	*	*	–	ESTONIAN AIR	–	–	2
(Chartair European Avn)	–	*	–	EURALAIR	–	–	3
CHILEAN AIR FORCE	–	–	1	(Europe Aero Service)	*	–	*
CHINA A/L	–	3	–	(EAS Europe A/L)	*	–	*
(CAAC)	*	–	–	(Euro Belgian A/L)	*	*	–
CHINA EASTERN A/L	3	–	–	(EuroBerlin)	*	–	–
CHINA GENERAL AVN	2 + 1	–	–	(European A/L)	*	–	–
CHINA NAT. AV. Corp	3	–	–	(European Air Transport/DHL)	*	–	–
CHINA SOUTHERN A/L	23	–	11	(Excalibur Awys)	*	–	–
CHINA SOUTHWEST A/L	20			FALCON AVN	3	–	–
CHINA UNITED A/L	6	–	–	FISCHER AIR	3	–	–
CHINA XINHUA A/L	6	3	–	FLIGHT WEST A/L	–	1	–
CHINA XINJIANG A/L	4	–	–	FREEDOM AIR INT'L	1	–	–
CHINA YUNNAN A/L	14	–	–	FRONTIER A/L	8 + 1	–	–
(Chinese Government)	*	–	–	FUJIAN A/L	–	–	1

Airline	-300	-400	-500
FUTURA A/L	*	11	–
GARUDA INDONESIA	4 + 2	7	4
GB AWYS	4	5	–
GERMANIA	9	–	–
GO FLY	6 + 7	–	–
GRAND AIR	0 + 2	–	–
GUANGXI A/L	–	–	1
GUIZHOU A/L	1 + 2	–	–
HAINAN A/L	7	5 + 1	–
(Hang Khong Vietnam)	*	–	–
HAPAG–LLOYD	*	9	3
(Hispania)	*	–	–
(Iberia)	*	–	–
ICELANDAIR	1	4	–
(Indotik Awys)	*	–	–
(Inter European Awys)	*	*	–
ISTANBUL A/L	2	6 + 2	–
ITT FLIGHT OPERATIONS	–	1	–
JAPAN AIR LINES	–	5	–
JAPAN TRANSOCEAN AIR	–	9 + 4	–
JET AWYS	2	13 + 1	2
JAT – YUGOSLAV A/L	7	–	–
KENYA AWYS	2 + 1	–	–
(Kiwi Travel Int'l)	–	*	–
KLM	18	19	–
(Ladeco)	*	–	–
L'AEROPOSTALE	15	–	–
LAUDA AIR	2	2	–
LAM	*	–	–
(Linjeflyg)	*	–	*
LITHUANIAN A/L	1	–	–
LAB – LLOYD AERO BOLIVIANO	1	–	–
LOT – POLISH A/L	2	7	6
LUFTHANSA	46	*	30

Airline	-300	-400	-500
LUXAIR	–	2	4
MACEDONIAN A/L	1	–	–
MAERSK AIR	9	*	14
MAERSK AIR UK	–	–	4
MALAYSIA A/L	2	39	9
MALEV	4	2	2 + 5
(Markair)	*	*	–
MEXICAN AF	1	–	–
(Modiluft)	–	*	–
(Monarch A/L)	*	–	–
(Morris Air)	*	–	–
MYANMAR AWYS INT'L	–	2	–
(New York Air)	*	–	–
NORDESTE	–	–	2
(Nordic East Awys)	*	*	–
NORDIC EUROPEAN A/L	1	*	–
(Noroeste)	–	–	*
(Nortjet)	–	*	–
(Norway A/L)	*	–	–
Air Europe Scandinavia)			
(Novair)	–	*	–
(Odyssey Int'l)	*	–	–
OLYMPIC AWYS	2	13	–
(Oman Air)	*	–	–
(Orbi)	*	–	–
(Orion Awys)	*	–	–
(Pacific A/L)	*	–	–
(Pacific Express)	*	–	–
PAKISTAN INT'L A/L	7	–	–
PAN AM	–	*	–
PEGASUS A/L	–	8	–
PERUVIAN AIR FORCE	–	–	1
PHILIPPINE A/L	10	–	–
(Philippine Government)	*	–	–
(Piedmont A/L)	*	*	–

Airline	-300	-400	-500
PLUNA	*	–	–
POLYNESIAN A/L	1	–	–
PRINCESS A/L	1	–	–
PRIVATAIR	1	–	1
PRO AIR	–	2 + 1	–
QANTAS	16	22	–
REPUBLIC of KOREA AF	1	–	–
RIO SUL	–	–	10 + 2
(Royal Air Cambodge)	–	*	–
ROYAL AIR MAROC	*	7	6
ROYAL THAI AF	*	1	–
ROYAL TONGAN A/L	1	*	–
RYAN INT'L	*	*	*
(Saarland Air)	*	–	–
SABENA	6	3	6
SAETA – AIR ECUADOR	1	–	–
SAHARA INDIA A/L	*	4	–
SAS – SCANDINAVIAN A/L	–	–	*
SATA – AIR ACORES	2	–	–
(Schreiner Awys)	*	–	–
SHAMEEN AIR	–	1	–
SHANDONG A/L	4 + 2	–	–
SHANGHAI A/L	1	–	–
SHENZHEN A/L	6	–	–
SIERRA PACIFIC A/L	*	–	–
SILKAIR	4	–	1
(Singapore A/L)	*	–	–
SOBELAIR	1	3	–
SOLOMONS A/L	1	*	–
(South East European A/L/Virgin)	–	*	–
(South Korean Government)	*	–	–
SOUTHWEST A/L	190	–	25
(Star Europe)	*	*	–
STERLING A/L	2		1

Airline	-300	-400	-500
(Sudflug)	*	–	–
(Sultan Air)	*	–	–
SUN EXPRESS	3	2	–
(Sunworld Int'l Awys)	*	–	–
TACA INT'L	1	–	–
(TAEA)	*	–	–
TAESA	3	2	*
TAP – AIR PORTUGAL	7	–	–
TAROM	5 + 1	–	–
(TAT European A/L)	*	–	–
THAI AWYS INT'L	–	13	–
(Time Air Sweden)	*	–	–
(Tradewinds)	*	–	–
TRANSAVIA	12	*	–
TRANSBRASIL	6	4	–
(TEA – Trans European Awys)	*	–	–
TEA CYPRUS	*	–	–
(TEA France)	*	–	–
(TEA Italy)	*	–	–
(TEA Switzerland)	*	–	–
(TEA UK)	*	–	–
(Transglobal)	–	*	–
(Transmed)	*	*	–
(Transpacific Air)	–	–	*
WINAIR	3	–	–
TRANSWEDE	1	–	–
TRANS SERVICE	–	1	–
TUNIS AIR	*	–	4
THY – TURKISH A/L	–	28	2
TURKMENISTAN A/L	3	–	–
UGANDA A/L	–	–	1
UKRAINE INT'L A/L	2 + 1	0 + 2	–
UNITED A/L	101	–	57
(Universair)	*	–	–
(USAir)	*	*	–

Airline	-300	-400	-500
US AWYS	85	54	–
VANGUARD A/L	*	–	–
VARIG	30 + 1	–	–
VASP	2	–	–
VIRGIN EXPRESS	11 + 2	5	–
(Viva Air)	*	–	–
(Western Pacific A/L)	*	–	–
WUHAN A/L	7	–	–
XIAMEN A/L	–	–	7
YEMENIA	*	–	–
ZHONGYUAN A/L	3	–	–

Airline	-600	-700	-800	-900
AB A/L	–	0 + 6	–	–
AIR ALGERIE	0 + 3	–	0 + 7	–
AIR BERLIN	–	–	3 + 5	–
AIR CHINA	–	–	0 + 7	–
AIR EUROPA	–	–	0 + 10	–
AIR PACIFIC	–	1	0 + 2	–
ALASKA A/L	–	0 + 8	–	0 + 10
AMERICAN A/L	–	–	0 + 100	–
ATLAS AIR CARGO	–	0 + 1	–	–
BRAATHENS	–	3 + 9	–	–
BRITANNIA AB	–	–	1 + 5	–
CHINA A/L	–	–	5 + 1	–
CHINA S/WEST A/L	–	–	0 + 3	–
CHINA XINJIANG A/L	–	0 + 3	–	–
CHINA YUNNAN A/L	–	0 + 4	–	–
CONDOR	–	1	–	–
CONTINENTAL A/L	0 + 30	16 + 20	10 + 32	0 + 15
CRONUS	–	0 + 1	–	–
DELTA A/L	–	–	5 + 76	–
EASTWIND A/L	–	2	–	–
EASYJET	–	0 + 15	–	–
EASYJET SWIT.	–	1	–	–

Airline	-600	-700	-800	-900
EL AL	–	0 + 2	0 + 3	–
EURALAIR	–	–	0 + 2	–
GERMANIA	–	9 + 3	–	–
HAINAN A/L	–	–	2 + 3	–
HAPAG–LLOYD	–	–	6 + 15	–
ISRAIR	–	0 + 2	–	–
JET AWYS	–	0 + 4	2 + 7	–
KLM	–	–	0 + 8	0 + 4
KOREAN AIR	–	–	0 + 11	0 + 11
LAPA	–	2 + 13	–	–
LAUDA AIR	0 + 2	0 + 4	1 + 1	–
LOT – POLISH A/L	–	–	0 + 2	–
LTU	–	0 + 2	–	–
MAERSK AIR	–	3 +3	–	–
MALAYSIA A/L	–	0 + 1(BBJ)	–	–
NORTH AM. A/L	–	–	1	–
NOVAIR	–	–	0 + 2	–
OLYMPIC AWYS	–	–	0 + 8	–
PEGASUS A/L	–	–	0 + 1	–
PRIVATAIR	–	0 + 2(BBJ)	–	–
R.O.C.A.F.	–	–	0 + 1	–
ROYAL AIR MAROC	–	0 + 2	2 + 5	–
RYANAIR	–	–	0 + 25	–
SABRE AWYS	–	–	2 + 2	–
SAS – SCAND. A/L	9 + 46	–	–	–
SHANDONG A/L	–	–	0 + 2	–
SHANGHAI A/L	–	1 + 1	–	–
SHENZHEN A/L	–	2	–	–
SOUTHWEST A/L	–	16 + 113	–	–
STERLING EURO. A/L	–	–	2 + 3	–
(TEA Switzerland)	–	*	–	–
TRANSAERO	–	2	–	–
TRANSAVIA	–	–	3 +5	–
TUNISAIR	0 + 8	–	–	–
TURK HAVA YOLLARI	–	–	6 + 20	–

CUMULATIVE TOTALS AS AT NOVEMBER 1998

Airline	-600	-700	-800	-900
US NAVY	–	0 + 5	–	–
VARIG	–	0 + 9	0 + 10	–
VIRGIN EXPRESS	–	–	0 + 2	
XIAMEN A/L	–	4	–	–

Aircraft	Ord	Del'd
B737–100	30	30
B737–200	1,114	1,114
B737–300	1,104	1,076
B737–400	484	473
B737–500	387	383

Aircraft	Ord	Del'd
B737–600	135	9
B737–700	447	75
B737–800	459	51
B737–900	40	0
Total	**4,200**	**3,210**

ABOVE: Air Atlanta is an Icelandic charter airline formed in 1986 which is now a major L-1011 TriStar operator, particularly in the UK leisure market. The airline's fleet also includes Boeing 747s and 737s. Two of the latter type currently feature on the inventory, both are series -200s. In 1995 and 1996, however, the company operated a single 737-300 TF-ABK. The aircraft is seen during a visit to Gatwick wearing additional Aviareps titles.

BELOW: Formed as Abelag in 1979, Air Belgium's modest fleet comprises just two 737s, a -300 and a -400. Air Belgium operates mainly to the holiday destinations around the Mediterranean and to the Canary Islands. Leased Boeing 737-46B OO-ILJ was delivered to the airline new in July 1991 and is operated in an all-economy 170-seat configuration. This photograph was taken at Brussels in August 1996, since when the airline has introduced a new livery.

AIR BERLIN

TOP LEFT: Air Berlin's fleet of Boeing 737-400s continues to grow and now numbers nine aircraft, although most, if not all will be disposed of with the introduction of the six -800s on order. The 737-400 has proved an invaluable aircraft in the European leisure market with the capability of carrying a full load of passengers in high density configuration on four hours plus journeys to the Canary Islands. Photographed at its Berlin /Tegel base in May 1997 is 737-4K5 D-ADAB.

AIR CHARTER

BELOW LEFT: Air Charter is a subsidiary of Air France and uses aircraft leased from the parent company on inclusive and *ad hoc* charter work. The fleet presently comprises Airbus A320s and A300s, alongside a couple of elderly 737-200s. The Boeing 727s previously operated have since been disposed of, as has 737-53A F-GHXM which was once leased from and operated on behalf of EAS Europe Airlines.

AIR CALEDONIE

TOP: Air Caledonie International, the airline of the French protectorate of the same name has recently changed its name to AirCalin. From Noumea-La Tontouta it operates single examples of the Twin Otter and Boeing 737-300. The latter, series -33A F-ODGX was acquired new in June 1989 and is used regional destinations such as Auckland, New Zealand.

AIR COLUMBUS

ABOVE: Based at Funchal, Madeira, Air Columbus was formed in 1989 to take advantage of the growing number of European tourists vacationing on this Portuguese island in the Atlantic Ocean. Boeing 727s were used for a number of years until replaced in March 1992 by a pair of leased former Norway Airlines 737-300s. Illustrated at Gatwick in the carrier's innovative livery is 737-33A CS-TKC *Santa Maria*.

AIR EUROPA

Spain's Air Europa has expanded its 737 fleet considerably in recent years, and now numbers 12 -300s and six -400s. The airline was formed in 1986 to convey tourists from northern Europe to the Spanish resorts on the mainland as well as the Balearic and Canary Islands. The airline was largely unaffected by the demise of its UK cousin Air Europe, whose livery was identical.

ABOVE: Illustrated leaving Gatwick is a 737-3Q8 wearing the 'B' class registration EC-520.

BELOW: A few of Air Europa's 737s and 757s have recently been seen in a revised mainly white livery as seen on 737-3Y0 EC-GEQ at Madrid's Barajas airport.

AIR EUROPE

ABOVE: Formed in May 1979 Air Europe initially operated 737-200s on charter flights from Gatwick to the hotspots of the Mediterranean. The airline was however very ambitious and took delivery of new 737-300s and -400s, whilst inaugurating several schedules from Gatwick. Fokker F-100s and Boeing 757s were added to the inventory as was a Boeing 747, whilst orders were placed for MD-11s. It has been said that this rapid expansion contributed to the airline's downfall, though it was in fact due to the financial problems of its parent company, the International Leisure Group. Air Europe sadly ceased operations in May 1991, leaving the way open for BA to mop up the residue without any serious competition. Seen at the start of its take-off roll at Gatwick is 737-300 G-BMTF.

AIR FRANCE

BELOW: Air France, the French national carrier, received its first 737s, the series -200, in 1982. Since then the airline has bought from Boeing and added both the series -300 and -500, and currently operates six and 18 respectively on domestic and European routes. The -300s, including F-GHVN seen here at Gatwick, are all second-hand machines.

AIR HOLLAND

TOP LEFT: Air Holland began operations to work in the booming inclusive tour charter market in 1985 with a pair of Boeing 727s. These were disposed of some time ago, but the airline's fleet remains an all Boeing one, with three 737-300s and three 757s. The airline's livery is based on the colours of the Dutch flag, and look very pleasing indeed in the early morning sunshine on 737-3Y0 PH-OZB.

AIR MALAWAI

BELOW LEFT: The fleet inventory comprises three aircraft; a Do-228, an ATR-42 and a Boeing 737-300. The latter links Malawi's capital Blantyre with several important regional African cities, including Cape Town, Durban and Johannesburg in South Africa. The single 737, series -33A 7Q-YKP *Kwacha* was acquired in May 1991 and is configured with 19 business and 112 economy seats. It is seen at Johannesburg's Jan Smuts airport.

AIR MALTA

ABOVE: The island of Malta has long been popular with European tourists and Air Malta has successfully tapped into this. From its inception with second-hand equipment in 1973 the airline now boasts a modern fleet of Airbus, Boeing and British Aerospace types. The airline's 737 fleet comprises three -200s and three -300s. Of the latter, 9H-ABT is seen on roll-out after landing at Gatwick. The appearance of the engine nacelle being split in two denotes that the thrust reversers are deployed.

AIR NIPPON

Formerly known as Nihon Kinyori Airways, Air Nippon is an associate company of All Nippon Airways, and the livery of the larger carrier adorns the airline's aircraft. The first 737, a series -200 was acquired from All Nippon in 1983, with others following. These are now being replaced by new series -500s, whose numbers will total 14. Photographed during flight tests at Boeing Field is 737-54K JA8595. *Matthew Martin*

AIR PACIFIC

RIGHT: Fiji's Air Pacific has one of the most colourful liveries of any 737 operator. The airline uses single examples of the 737-300 and -500 on regional services from Nadi, supplemented by a single 767. Long haul flights to Honolulu and Los Angeles are flown by a Boeing 747-200 leased from Qantas. Photographed at Auckland is 737-5Y0 DQ-FJB named *Island of Taveuni*. The airline has three 737-700s on order with deliveries due to commence in October 1998.

AIR ONE

BELOW: Known formerly as Aliadriatica, Air One is certainly making its presence felt. The low cost carrier is attracting large numbers of passengers on the busy Rome–Milan route, and has made inroads into Alitalia's load factors on a route it once dominated. Air One has also started international services with a thrice daily Milan–London/Stansted service. Four ex-Lufthansa 737-400s are augmented by six 737-300s and four 737-200s. Photographed on the taxiway at Rome's Fiumicino airport in September 1997 is the recently delivered former Lufthansa 737-430 D-ABKK, now carrying the Irish registration EI-COJ.

AIR PROVENCE CHARTER

BELOW RIGHT: Air Provence Charter is a joint venture between Euro Belgian Airlines and Air Provence International. It operates three Boeing 737s leased from the Belgian carrier, two -300s in basic Euro Belgian livery and one -400 operated jointly with Virgin Express in that carrier's livery.

AIR UKRAINE

FOLLOWING PAGES: Air Ukraine International was founded in 1992 with a pair of Boeing 737-400s leased from GPA. Subsequently these aircraft were joined by a single series -300, and later a pair of -200s, as the lease rates on the -400s proved too expensive. There was considerable confusion outside its home country between Air Ukraine International and Air Ukraine, once the Kiev Directorate of Aeroflot. Air Ukraine's tail logo was virtually identical, so to avoid this confusion Air Ukraine International changed its name to Ukraine International Airlines and changed its tail logo. It disposed of the -300 but increased traffic resulted in the airline signing a lease agreement to add a -300 to its inventory again.

MAIN PICTURE: UR-GAE, the first -300 operated. Compare the tail logo with that used earlier under the previous name.

INSET PHOTOGRAPH: Seen at Gatwick a few months after the November 1992 delivery is 737-4Y0 UR-GAA.

ALASKA AIRLINES

TOP: 737-490 N767AS climbs out of Anchorage into the crisp clear evening skies. Alaska uses 737-400s on routes linking Alaska with Seattle and the US west coast, while a few series -200Cs are used within the state.

ALOHA AIRLINES

BELOW: From their Honolulu base Aloha's 737 fleet is kept busy from dawn to dusk as they flit around the Hawaiian Islands. Due to the short sectors the planes record an impressive number of cycles during a working day. The corrosive volcanic soil on the islands combined with the salty air and high cycles were deemed responsible for an amazing incident on 28 April 1978. Series -200 N73711 suffered an in-flight structural failure in which the fuselage roof peeled back like a sardine can top. Amazingly the pilot managed to land the aircraft safely, the only loss of life being an unfortunate stewardess. Inspection of other aircraft in the fleet revealed three other aircraft of a similar age were also affected and they were withdrawn from service. The airline then acquired a few series -300s and, later, a pair of -400s. The latter's stay with the airline was short-lived, though another pair of this variant are currently on order. Illustrated taxying to the 'reef' runway at Honolulu is 737-497 N401AL.

AIR VANUATU

FAR LEFT: Photographed about to land at Sydney is Air Vanuatu Boeing 737-476 VH-TJI. This aircraft is leased from and operated jointly with Qantas, though when this photograph was taken in 1993 it is in partial livery of its owner Australian Airlines, which has since been taken over by Qantas. Air Vanuatu also operates a single EMB-110 Bandeirante from its Port Vila base.

AMERICA WEST AIRLINES

FOLLOWING PAGES: Recovering well after a financially difficult period, this airline's fleet is again showing signs of expansion, with a fleet of 42 737-300s forming the backbone of the inventory. They are supported by a smaller number of series -200s as well as 26 Airbus A320s while 14 757s are used on longer sectors.

MAIN PICTURE: America West's network has recently expanded and now covers 75 destinations in North America and Mexico. The airline has also recently introduced a new livery with the predominantly white scheme giving way to one of white and two shades of green. Displaying this livery is 737-3Y0 N323AW. This aircraft is on lease from GECAS and was acquired in February 1995 having previously served in Spain with Air Europa.

INSERT: The distinctive chocolate-brown hills surrounding Phoenix Sky Harbor airport provide a pleasing backdrop to 737-33A N166AW.

ANSETT AUSTRALIA
ABOVE LEFT: Featuring a rendition of the national flag on the tail, Ansett Australia 737-377 VH-CZE was photographed on approach to Sydney's Kingsford-Smith International airport in February 1993. Since then the airline has introduced a pleasant new tail logo and acquired three Boeing 747-300s on lease from Singapore Airlines to operate newly introduced long haul services.

ASIANA AIRLINES
LEFT: When Asiana Airlines was formed in December 1988 the carrier was not permitted to compete with Korean Air on international routes. This restriction was soon lifted however, and nearby Japan was the first country chosen. Tokyo and Nagoya were the first cities to be served, and it was at the latter where 737-4Y0 HL7258 was photographed in April 1990. Asiana's fleet and route network continue to expand at a phenomenal rate, 21 737-400s and four -500s will soon be in use, while Boeing 747s and 767s serve US and European destinations.

AUSTRALIAN AIRLINES
TOP: Previously known as Trans Australia Airlines, a name change simply to Australian Airlines in 1986 coincided with the delivery of the first of a batch of 16 Boeing 737-300s. These were followed in 1990 by series -400s, however in the autumn of 1993 the airline was taken over by flag carrier Qantas, leaving Ansett as the only real internal competitor. Photographed climbing out of Sydney a few months before the take-over is 737-476 VH-TJM.

BALKAN BULGARIAN AIRLINES
ABOVE: This airline acquired its first western equipment towards the end of 1990 with the lease of a pair of Boeing 737-500s. A third was added a year later, as were a quartet of Airbus A320s. The Airbuses have since been disposed of, but the Boeings soldier on alongside a large fleet of Tu-154s on European services. Climbing out of Amsterdam's Schiphol airport is 737-53A LZ-BOB named *City of Plovdiv.*

BRAATHENS

BELOW RIGHT: Braathens'
penchant for the annual painting
of special 'Sommerflyet' markings
on one of its aircraft is eagerly
awaited by aviation enthusiasts
around Europe, and in 1995 they
were not disappointed. Again 737-
505 LN-BRJ was the chosen
'canvas', for what is one of the
zaniest schemes yet. The aircraft
was captured on film on a summer's evening at the holding point
for Gatwick's runway 08R as it
awaits take-off clearance for Oslo's
Fornebu airport.

TOP RIGHT: Braathens' more
usual livery is seen here on 737-405
LN-BRQ as it rotates from
Gatwick bound for Bergen.
Braathens route network is
expanding throughout Europe,
with Amsterdam the next to be
served due to a link-up with KLM.
The airline's 737 fleet now comprises seven -400s and 24 -500s,
while 12 -700s are on order with
deliveries commencing in the first
quarter of 1998.

BRITISH MIDLAND

ABOVE: British Midland's new
livery is not unlike that of United
Airlines, the largest of the many
carriers with whom it code shares.
British Midland's 737 fleet has
expanded considerably and
currently comprises nine -300s, six
-400s and 13 -500s. The airline was
expected to be a customer for the
Next Generation 737, but has
opted for Airbus A320s and A321s
instead. Photographed taxying to
its gate at Glasgow is brand new
737-300 G-ODSK.

BRITISH AIRWAYS

British Airways bid for world domination soon spread beyond home shores when it bought a majority shareholding in Friedrichshafen based Delta Air. The airline has since been renamed Deutsche BA, and with a fleet of Fokker F-100s and Boeing 737-300s is now a major player in the German internal market. In the last couple of years the airline has introduced services to London and Gatwick from Berlin, Hamburg and Munich, though the aircraft are also used for some weekend charter work.

RIGHT: Photographed taxying to its gate at Gatwick is 737-L9 D-ADBF, one of 10 leased from Maersk Air. Although rumours were rife, the first inkling of the new British Airways colour scheme was in January 1997 when a couple of Deutsche BA 737s appeared in what is known as the interim scheme. This scheme is the basis for the new livery, so that when the day for unveiling the new livery came it wouldn't take too long to paint the tail and complete the scheme.

FAR RIGHT: Climbing into the crisp winter skies in the interim scheme is 737-3L9 D-ADBB. Deutsche BA is in the process of taking delivery of six new -300s to add to the 12 already in use, while a single -400 is currently leased from Nordic European. When the present batch of 737s are delivered the Fokker F-100s will be returned to TAT from whom they are leased.

ABOVE: When France's TAT European Airlines became yet another British Airways subsidiary a number of the airline's Fokker F-28 and F-100 aircraft were repainted in BA livery. In March 1996 two former TransBrasil Boeing 737-300s were acquired for use on services to Heathrow and Gatwick, and these too were quickly attired in BA markings. Seen at Gatwick soon after entering service is 737-3Y0 F-GLLD. Note the Air UK Leisure 737-400 in the background.

ABOVE LEFT: British Airways now has 20 737-400s based at Gatwick, however this includes a mixture of series -436 aircraft delivered to the airline direct and -400s which were on lease to Dan-Air at the time of the take-over of that airline. To the uninitiated this may not sound a problem, but for the airline's crew schedulers it is. Unlike the leased examples, the series -436 aircraft have analogue engine instruments which BA insisted on in the aftermath of the British Midland crash. Until a pilot has completed the required course he is not allowed to crew a series -436, and this can cause nightmares for the schedulers. Unlike the Heathrow based -400s which are configured for 141 seats those at Gatwick have an extra row fitted so they can carry 147 passengers. Illustrated is G-DOCZ, the third last of the 737-436s to be delivered.

CARNIVAL AIR LINES

ABOVE: Based at Fort Lauderdale, Florida, one of the main aspects of Carnival Airlines is the task of conveying passengers to join the cruise ships of the Carnival Line. The fleet comprises Airbus A300 wide-bodies and Boeing 727s and 737s. The latter type includes a pair of -200s and seven series -400s. The latter fleet is sometimes augmented in winter time by similar types from European charter airlines. Photographed on approach to Los Angeles is 737-4Q8 N404KW.

CHINA NATIONAL AVIATION CORPORATION

RIGHT: The letters BC stand for Beijing Capital airport, however they could easily stand for Boeing Country, such is the proliferation of Boeing types, particularly the 737. Boeing's popular twin-jet has proved a favoured mount by most of the country's airlines, including the China National Aviation Corporation who have three in use, all on lease from China Southwest. Seen on push-back from its gate at Beijing is 737-3Z0 B-2957.

CAYMAN AIRWAYS

ABOVE RIGHT: Photographed about to depart Miami in 1990 is 737-4Y0 VR-CAB belonging to Cayman Airways. This aircraft was one of two leased -400s operated, but these have since been disposed of in favour of a pair of older series -200s whose lease rates are no doubt considerably cheaper. The airline operates 737s from Georgetown to several US destinations, notably nearby Florida airports Miami and Tampa.

AIR CHINA

TOP: The Civil Aviation Administration of China (CAAC) is the regulatory aviation body in China, just like the CAA in the United Kingdom and the FAA in the United States. However at one time it was also the only airline, both for domestic and international services. It has been a strong supporter of Boeing products, and took delivery and operated 16 Boeing 737-200s, as well as a batch of -300s. When it was forced to abandon its role as an airline these aircraft were handed down to some of the many of the airlines now operating in this vast country. The current livery of Air China differs very little from that worn by CAAC aircraft, evidence of which is visible on 737-3J6 B-2531, which was delivered to CAAC in 1986 and transferred to Air China in May 1988.

CHINA XINHUA AIRLINES

ABOVE: Also based at Beijing's Capital airport is China Xinhua Airlines with a fleet of six 737-300s and two -400s, with another of the latter variant on order. Taxiing for departure on a crisp spring day is the airline's first 737, series -341 B-2908.

CHINA YUNNAN AIRLINES

TOP RIGHT: Kunmimg based China Yunnan Airlines was formed in 1992 with four 737-300s. Today the 737 fleet has increased to 11 with a further example on order, while three 767s have become more recent additions to the inventory. Taxiing for departure at Beijing in the airline's distinctive green and white livery is 737-3W0 B-2538.

CONDOR FLUGDIENST

CENTRE RIGHT: Lufthansa subsidiary Condor Flugdienst is Germany's largest charter airline, and has a growing fleet of Boeing 757s, 767s and DC-10s. The airline is the launch customer for the new lengthened 757-300 and has six A320s on order, the latter to form the new subsidiary Condor Berlin. With the arrival of the Airbus machines the four Boeing 737-300s (which it has on lease from Germania) will be disposed of. Sporting the company's bright yellow fin, 737-330 D-ABWA prepares to depart the sunshine of Las Palmas.

CONTINENTAL AIRLINES

BELOW RIGHT: The fortunes of Continental Airlines have taken an amazing about-turn over the past 12 months. Early in 1996 the airline was faced with severe financial difficulties due to its poor performance and it was noted for the cancellation of a number of aircraft on order. Under their chief executive Gordon Bethune the airline is completely revitalised, making huge profits and receiving plaudits for their standards of service. Furthermore orders have now been placed for a number of aircraft including Boeing 767s and 777s, though the airline continues to purchase good second-hand DC-10-30s to cope with steady expansion.

The airline has a sizeable fleet of 737s, which still includes 13 very elderly -100s and 17 -200s. It is new generation types which predominate however; 65 series -300s and 41 -500s, with a further 26 of the latter to be delivered. The airline has placed a substantial order for Next Generation 737s, comprising 30 -600s, 26 -700s and 22 -800s. Wearing the titling of the now discarded low cost Continental Lite operation at Cleveland is 737-524 N17619.

CORSAIR

LEFT: A Paris-Orly based charter operator with an increasing participation in the long haul market. To cater for this the airline's Boeing 747 fleet has been increased to six aircraft of four different variants, ranging from the SP to the -300. These are joined by a pair of DC-10s, whilst two 737-200s and two -400s are used on European routes. One of the latter, 737-4B3 F-GFUG was photoed shortly after take-off showing the current livery, known as the 'Dulux' scheme, in reference to the well-known paint maker.

CZECH AIRLINES

BOTTOM LEFT: Like many airlines in Eastern Europe CSA Czech Airlines has gradually disposed of most of the Soviet-built airliners on its inventory in favour of western machines. Although a small number of Tu-134s and Tu-154s are still in use it is the Boeing 737 which operate the vast majority of European services. Five series -500s were acquired between June and August 1992, and a further three have since been added plus two more on order. A pair of leased -400s joined the fleet in spring of 1995, one of these is OK-WGF seen here on approach to Heathrow. A further three are due.

DAN-AIR

BELOW: Dan-Air began operations in 1953 and soon had a diverse fleet of aircraft. In the 1970s it was the largest Comet 4 operator as it built up its charter network out of Gatwick. Later the scheduled network became more important and was operated mainly with BAe 111s and later 146s, as well as Boeing 737s. By 1992 the airline's fleet had grown to over 50 aircraft which also included BAe 748s and Boeing 727s. In 1992 the airline suffered from financial problems and eventually fell to a take-over by British Airways with its leased 737-400s and route network subsumed into BAs operation. At rest in its final days in Dan-Air livery is 737-3Q8 G-BNNJ, which went on to serve with Excalibur Airways.

DELTA AIRLINES

FAR LEFT: The Olympic Mountains provide a pleasant background to Delta Airlines 737-347 N306WA as it taxies clear of the runway at Seattle-Tacoma airport with a United Airlines example close on its heels. Delta acquired 13 of these aircraft from Western Airlines when it took over that carrier in April 1987. Delta also has 54 -200s on its inventory.

EGYPTAIR

BOTTOM LEFT: There are few 737 new generation operators in Africa, and most are strung along the northern coast of the continent, namely Egypt, Morocco and Tunisia. Egyptair acquired the first of six 737-200s in 1975, which have largely been replaced by five series -500s, the first of which was delivered in April 1991. Photographed at Geneva is 737-566 SU-GBK *Kalabsha*.

EASYJET

LEFT: Newcomer on the British aviation scene is easyJet which works from its base at uncrowded Luton airport north of London. The fledgling airline has certainly made an impact in the UK and Europe — with its no-frills service easyJet offers fares much lower than its competitors — the tactics worked as airlines such as Air UK, British Airways and British Midland have since been forced to reduce fares considerably on the routes from London to Aberdeen, Edinburgh and Glasgow. This low cost airline also quickly introduced services to Amsterdam and Nice, with the former in particular proving very successful. The initial two 737-200 have now been disposed of, and five -300s are currently in use with another imminent. The airline has also announced an order for a further 12 direct from Boeing. Photographed taxying for departure from its Luton base is G-EZYA, the airline's first series -300.

EURO BELGIAN AIRLINES

BELOW: 737-3M8 OO-LTL about to land on runway 02 at its Brussels base on 20 August 1996 — the day the first 737 appeared in the colours of Virgin Express. Most of the carrier's aircraft have now been repainted in the vivid red and white colours of its new identity.

EUROBERLIN FRANCE

ABOVE: Formed in late 1988 in a joint venture between Air France and Lufthansa, as the latter was not permitted to operate domestic services from Berlin. From its base at Tegel airport the airline operated to a number of major German cities using six Boeing 737-300s provided and operated by Monarch Airlines. The airline ceased operations on 31 October 1994, when Lufthansa was permitted to operate these services. Seen taxying for departure at Tegel is 737-3Y0 G-MONH.

EXCALIBUR AIRWAYS

BELOW: Formed on 1 May 1992 when it acquired the assets of TEA (UK). A fleet of four Airbus A320s was acquired on lease, and although the airline was based at East Midlands the bulk of operations were from Gatwick. To cope with increasing demand a former Dan-Air 737-300 was acquired in March 1994, and registered G-OCHA. Despite plans to stop short haul and move into long haul operations, the airline ceased operations in the first quarter of 1996.

FALCON AVIATION
ABOVE: A Malmo-based airline which has been in business since 1986, Falcon used to operate Lockheed Electras, but now utilises a fleet of three Boeing 737-300s fitted with a cargo door on freight, *ad hoc* and inclusive tour charters. In passenger configuration the aircraft has 142 seats. Displaying the company's rather insipid livery at Stockholm's Arlanda airport is 737-33A(QC) SE-DPB *Pilgrimsfalken.*

FRONTIER AIRLINES
BELOW: This Denver based airline features large transfers of American animals and birds on the tails of its aircraft. The airline has an all 737 fleet, comprising seven series -200 and six -300s, with a further one of the latter due. In July 1997 Frontier announced that it was to merge with Western Pacific Airlines based at nearby Colorado Springs. By the end of September, however, in a surprise announcement it was disclosed that the merger plans had been terminated, furthermore the recently agreed codeshare was also to be terminated. Photographed about to land at Los Angeles in September 1996 is 737-317 EI-CHH. This aircraft is leased from GECAS and features a mallard duck on the port side of the fin, while the starboard side features a mustang.

FUTURA

TOP LEFT: Spanish charter operator Futura introduced a twice weekly scheduled Gatwick–Palma service to complement its extensive charter network. Futura started operations in February 1990 with financial backing from Aer Lingus, and its all 737-400 fleet has now expanded to 11 aircraft. Photographed at Geneva is EC-FLD.

GERMANIA

CENTRE LEFT: Like other German charter operators, Germania operates primarily to holiday destinations around the Mediterranean area with a fleet comprised exclusively of Boeing 737-300s. The airline has 13 on the inventory, though four and one are leased to fellow German operators Condor and Deutsche BA respectively. About to land at Heathrow for maintenance by BA is 737-3L9 D-AGEH.

HAINAN AIRLINES

BELOW LEFT: Hainan Island is situated off China's south coast to the south-west of Hong Kong. From its base at Haikou, the largest town on the island, Hainan Airlines operates a fleet of five 737-300s and four -400s. The airline is also about to take delivery of 12 SA227 Metroliners. Photographed at Beijing is 737-4Q8 B-2970. Delivered in August 1996, like the majority of the fleet, it is on lease from ILFC.

ICELANDAIR

ABOVE: Operating the 737-400 since April 1989 these aircraft are used on services linking Iceland with Europe. The Boeing 757 joined the inventory the following year, and supplements the 737s as well as undertaking flights to several US destinations. Climbing out of Schiphol airport is the airline's second 737-408, TF-FIB Eydis. Icelandair has just acquired a 737-300 freighter on lease from ILFC.

INTER EUROPEAN AIRWAYS

BELOW: A Cardiff based charter operator and a subsidiary of Aspro Holidays, the airline started operations with Boeing 737-200s, which were eventually replaced by series -300s and a -400. Expansion saw the airline acquire four Boeing 757s and a pair of A320s, however in 1993 the parent company was taken over by Airtours International, and their aircraft absorbed into the Airtours fleet. The Boeing 737s were returned to the lessor. Seen at Gatwick in October 1992 is 737-4S3 G-IEAE.

JUGOSLOVENSKI AEROTRANSPORT

MAIN PICTURE: JAT has had a troubled life in the past few years due to the civil war and unrest in the former Yugoslavia. Unable to operate, it leased out a number of aircraft but is now slowly returning to normal. As part of this rejuvenation it has introduced a new livery, as seen on 737-3H9 YU-ANI.

ISTANBUL AIRLINES

INSET LEFT: During the 1980s there was an explosion of tourism in Turkey, and several charter companies were formed, one being Istanbul Airlines. Initially running Caravelles, 727s, 737s and 757s now feature. The 737 fleet comprises four series -400s, including TC-AYA seen here decelerating after landing at Gatwick.

KLM

INSET RIGHT: Royal Dutch Airlines names its Boeing 737-400s after explorers, and
David Livingston's name appears on the nose of 737-406 PH-BTC. The airline has
taken its -400 fleet to 19 aircraft with the acquisition of the former Air UK Leisure
machines. It also has 18 series -300s and four Next Generation -800s on order.

L'AEROPOSTALE

TOP LEFT: L'Aeropostale utilises a fleet of 15 Boeing 737-300 (QC) aircraft. These are used primarily on night postal services, however in daytime they can be fitted with 147 seats and used for passengers. The aircraft are often used in the latter role on Air France services, usually on low yield routes. Photographed visiting Gatwick in May 1992 operating an Air France Strasbourg service is 737-33A(QC) F-GIXD.

LAUDA AIR

CENTRE LEFT: Formed in 1979 to operate charter services with a pair of Fokker F-27s, since then Lauda has expanded considerably with scheduled services starting in 1988. The first Boeing 777 arrived in September 1997 to supplement 767s to the Far East and Australia, while Boeing 737s and Canadair Regional Jets are used on the European network. The 737 fleet comprises two -300s and two -400s with a pair of -800s on order. Featuring the airline's new livery with light grey upper surfaces instead of white is 737-3Z9 OE-ILF.

LOT

BOTTOM LEFT: Polish Airlines selected the Boeing 737 to replace its ageing fleet of Tu-134 and Tu-154 jets. It took delivery of the first of six new -500s in December 1992, though prior to those aircraft being ready it leased several of the type from Linjeflyg of Sweden. The company has since received seven series -400s and, to make up for a shortfall in capacity, acquired three -300s on lease in 1997, the latter primarily for use in the leisure market to Mediterranean resorts. In late 1998 these will be supplemented by a pair of -800s which are on order. Illustrated is 737-45D SP-LLC.

LUFTHANSA

ABOVE: Europe's largest 737 operator with a fleet comprising 47 -300s and 30 -500s. Seven -400s acquired in 1992 proved unsuitable to the route network and all were disposed of by mid 1997. Illustrated in Lufthansa's old livery is 737-330 D-ABXR.

LUXAIR

BELOW: Luxair uses a pair of 737-400s and four -500s on its jet network throughout Europe. Both variants are in one-class configuration, the -400 seating 158 passengers and the -500 121 passengers. Embraer EMB-120 and Fokker F-50 turboprops serve regional destinations and thinner routes. Photographed inbound to Heathrow is 737-5C9 LX-LGO.

MAERSK AIR

ABOVE LEFT: Birmingham-based Maersk Air (UK) has recently replaced some of its BAe111s with three Boeing 737-500s handed down from the parent company. Being a British Airways franchise carrier these aircraft operate in full BA livery, all three aircraft sporting different tail designs as part of the BA world image scheme, which received mixed reviews. Seen taxying to its gate at Birmingham is 737-5L9 G-MSKC wearing the 'Waves of the City' design. This aircraft was formerly OY-MAE with Maersk Air.

MALEV

LEFT: Malev was one of the first eastern European airlines to break with tradition and order airliners from the west. Three Boeing 737-200s were leased from GPA at the end of 1988, and these have since been followed by four -300s and a pair of -400s. These aircraft have taken over most of the European routes previously operated by Tu-154s. The airline's first -300 series aircraft was HA-LED seen here on approach to runway 27L at Heathrow.

MONARCH AIRLINES

TOP: Photographed at Glasgow in 1988 is 737-300 G-BNXW . Monarch has been a 737 operator since 1980 when it received its first -200. The airline soon built up a large fleet of 737-300s, including some which were operated on behalf of EuroBerlin France. In recent years the company's 757s have been supplemented by Airbus A320s, and an A321 joined the fleet in 1997. This was the year when the airline's last 737-300 departed for pastures new, joining easyJet at Luton.

MORRIS AIR

ABOVE: Formed in 1992, Salt Lake City based Morris Air was a successful low cost operator serving niche routes which the larger carriers ignored. The airline quickly built up its Boeing 737-300 fleet to around 20 aircraft. Its success however attracted interest from Southwest Airlines, whose offer proved too good to turn down, and Morris Air was taken over by Southwest on 31 December 1993. Morris's aircraft and routes were subsumed into Southwest by mid-1995. Photographed in February 1993 at Seattle-Tacoma is series -300 N319AW.

MYANMAR AIRWAYS INTERNATIONAL

LEFT: Seen about to land at Hong Kong's Kai Tak airport is 737-4H6 9M-MMH belonging to Myanmar Airways International. The airline was formed in 1993 and the initial equipment comprised a Boeing 757 leased from Royal Brunei. Towards the end of 1994 a pair of 737-400s were acquired on lease from Malaysia Airlines, and these are still used on regional routes from Yangon — formerly known as Rangoon.

NORDIC EUROPEAN AIRLINES

BELOW LEFT: Nordic East Airlines was formed in 1991 as a charter operator and specifically set to work to try and capture some of the growing number of Scandinavians heading for the winter sunshine of the southern Mediterranean and the Canary Islands. The small fleet ultimately comprised three 737 — all different variants — and a pair of Lockheed L-1011 TriStars. Early in 1997 the airline changed its name to Nordic European Airlines. Photographed in Nordic East titling in 1996 about to land at Athens is 737-4Y0 SE-DTB; this aircraft is currently leased to Deutsche BA in an all white scheme.

OLYMPIC AIRWAYS

BELOW: Olympic Airways association with the Boeing 737 dates back to 1975 when the first of 11 -200s were delivered. These aircraft still soldier on working domestic and European services, but are now supported by seven -400s, the first of which was delivered in September 1991. The airline has just announced an order for four -800s and intends to take more of the variant to replace the elderly 737-200 and 727-200s. Lining up for departure from runway 33R at Athens is 737-484 SX-BKB *Olynthos*.

POLYNESIAN AIRLINE

TOP LEFT: This Samoan airline has operated a single leased 737-300 since September 1992 to link the capital Apia with Auckland, Christchurch, Melbourne, Nadi, Rarotonga, Suva, Sydney, Tongatupu and Wellington. The trusty BN-2 Islander and DHC-6 Twin Otter are used on inter-island services. Photographed taxying for departure at Auckland is 737-3Q8 5W-ILF. This plane was the subject of an unusual incident a few years ago when the starboard undercarriage would not lower, forcing a landing at Apia which caused some damage to the starboard wing and engine pod. It transpired the failure of the landing gear was caused by the body of a stowaway in the undercarriage bay which jammed the mechanism.

RIO SUL

CENTRE LEFT: Throughout South America there are many 737 operators but only a few use the new generation series — the older -200 being the most widely used in the continent. Most of the new generation types are operated in Brazil with four different airlines. Although formed in 1976 as a Varig subsidiary it was October 1992 when Rio Sul received its first jet, a brand new 737-500. The airline now has 10 of these with two more on order. Presenting the airline's pleasant livery at Rio de Janeiro's downtown Santos Dumont airport is 737-5YO PT-SLT.

SAS SCANDINAVIAN AIRLINES

BELOW LEFT: SAS acquired its fleet of 737-500s by default due to the January 1993 take-over of domestic carrier Linjeflyg. The aircraft obviously did not fit into SAS's fleet which comprised some 100 DC-9 and MD-80 variants, and by February 1994 the first of the type was transferred on lease to partner British Midland. The remainder of the fleet has since travelled in the same direction, which makes the airline's decision to order 41 Next Generation -600s somewhat remarkable. Photographed at Stockholm's Arlanda airport during its brief spell in SAS livery is 737-59D SE-DNB *Birger Viking*.

ROYAL AIR MAROC

BELOW: This airline has the distinction of being the largest 737 operator in Africa. The airline took delivery of the first of seven -200s in 1975, followed by seven -400s from July 1990. To add to the family six -500s have been delivered, while nine -800s are currently on order for 1998 delivery. Photographed at Paris-Orly is 737-4B6 CN-RMG, the livery includes titling in English on the starboard side and in Arabic on the port.

ROYAL TONGAN AIRLINES

ABOVE: Like many carriers in the region Royal Tongan Airlines primarily operates inter-island services. These are operated by a pair of DHC-6 Twin Otters and a BAe748. Providing the islands' link with Australia and New Zealand is a single Boeing 737. This was a series -400 operated jointly with Solomons Airlines whose livery it sported. However since January 1995 an agreement was reached with Air Pacific, using one of that carrier's 737-300s (DQ-FJD), but featuring Air Pacific livery on the port side and Royal Tongan on the starboard. That aircraft is seen during a visit to Christchurch in November 1995.

ABENA BELGIAN WORLD AIRLINES

OP LEFT: Another long established European 737 operator, Sabena received the rst of 13 -200s back in April 1974. They are still in use today, though now support-d by a fleet of -300s, -400s and -500s. The airline operates six, three and six respec-vely of these new generation variants. Sabena has undergone a fleet rationalisation ecently with the A310s and DC-10s being replaced by A330s and A340s. A large umber of Avro RJ85 and RJ100s are being delivered to replace Fokker F-28s. hotographed in the airline's old livery at the holding point for runway 02 at russels is 737-329 OO-SDY.

ELOW LEFT: Featuring Sabena's new livery is 737-329 OO-SDV. To promote its artnership with Swissair the aircraft sports 'Flying together with Swissair' logo on e rear fuselage.

SHANDONG AIRLINES

BELOW: A small Chinese independent, Shandong's fleet comprises just three 737-300s and a single Yun Y-7. Photographed at Beijing is 737-35N B-2962. This aircraft was delivered in March 1996 in an all-economy 141-seat configuration.

SATA AIR ACORES

ABOVE: Operating on inter-island services between the Azores, SATA's home base is at Ponta Delgada, on San Miguel. In October 1985 SATA leased a Boeing 737-300 to link the islands with Lisbon, complementing TAP Air Portugal. Indeed some of the latter's services are now operated by SATA. During 1996 SATA also used the aircraft on a Gatwick–Lisbon service. CS-TGP *Corvo*, a 737-3Q8 formerly operated by EBA, is seen here at Horta on the island of Faial.

SINGAPORE AIRLINES

TOP: From November 1992 until it was sold in 1996 Singapore Airlines operated a single Boeing 737-300 freighter for use on some regional routes to augment its ever expanding fleet of 747 freighters. The freight door is clearly visible on the forward fuselage of 737-3M8 (F) 9V-SQZ as it commences its take-off roll at Kai Tak for the daily early morning departure for Singapore.

SOBELAIR

ABOVE: A subsidiary of Sabena, Sobelair operates charters throughout the Mediterranean with a fleet of Boeing 737s, and acquired 767s to operate across the Atlantic and to the Far East. The livery used to mirror that of Sabena, only in green rather than blue — later it changed to Sabena's blue, with only title differences. It followed suit with Sabena's new livery, but with the titles of both carriers. Featuring Sabena's blue livery but Sobelair titles is 737-46B OO-SBJ *Juliette*.

STAR EUROPE

TOP: Paris-Orly based Star Europe is France's newest charter airline, formed as recently as 1995. The first aircraft was 737-33A F-GRSA. This aircraft has since been disposed of, though a pair of -400s are currently used alongside a pair of new Airbus A320s acquired in the summer of 1997.

SOLOMONS AIRLINES

ABOVE: Solomons Airlines was formed in 1968 to operate inter-island services. The single 737 links Honiara's Henderson International airport with Auckland, Brisbane, Nadi and Port Vila. These services are operated by a 737-300 leased from, and operated jointly with Qantas. Prior to the current arrangement a leased 737-400 was operated jointly with Royal Tongan. The aircraft was, H4-SOL *Guadalcanal*, was photographed at Auckland in March 1993.

SOUTHWEST AIRLINES

Southwest Airlines has been a phenomenal success story. Since it was founded in 1967 the airline has gone from strength to strength and continues to expand and record massive profits. The airline was the original low cost no frills airline, and has been so successful that numerous competitors and start-ups have tried to emulate the formula — and many, such as Continental Lite have failed in the attempt. The airline's recipe for success can be put down to several factors, not least the enthusiasm and loyalty of the staff — a factor that the management of several major airlines such as British Airways should perhaps be looking at. Administration costs are a fraction of those of their competitors due to factors such as a simplified fare structure, re-usable plastic boarding cards, no pre-assigned seating and no interline baggage agreements. As no meals are served on board this also enables turn-round times to be kept to a minimum, usually around 20 minutes.

RIGHT: Southwest is the largest operator of the -300 with 186 of the type in use, some of which are painted in special colours. Phoenix is the airline's busiest hub where -300 N609SW *California One* awaits push-back clearance while another in standard livery taxies to its gate.

ABOVE AND BELOW: Other 737-300s in special colours of US States served by the airline include N383SW *Arizona One* and N352SW *Lone Star One*. The latter denotes the star on the Texas flag.

TACA INTERNATIONAL AIRLINES
TOP LEFT: El Salvador's TACA International Airlines has been a 737 operator since 1978. The airline's 737 fleet currently comprises 10 -200s and five -300s, all of which are leased. Series -300 N374TA was photographed about to land at Miami in January 1997. The airport is served several times a day by both 737 types.

TAROM
CENTRE LEFT: Tarom was the last of the major eastern European national carriers to buy Boeing with the acquisition of five -38Js in 1993 and 1994. Despite these additions to its fleet the airline still operates the elderly BAe111s and Tu-154s. Photographed on its approach to Heathrow is YR-BGB named *Bucaresti*.

TEA SWITZERLAND
BOTTOM LEFT: Formed as TEA Basel in 1988 this charter operator is now known as TEA Switzerland and uses the radio callsign "TopSwiss". It operates a fleet of five 737-300s, with a further example on order. The airline was an early customer for the 737-700, two of which are due very soon. Photographed about to depart Gatwick is 737-3Y0 HB-IID, an aircraft TEA recently disposed of.

THAI AIRWAYS INTERNATIONAL
ABOVE: Fast growing Thai Airways International selected the 737-400 for use on a number of domestic routes for which the Airbus A300 was proving too big. The first was delivered in August 1990 and a further four were delivered in August 1997 to take the total to 11. Seen at its Bangkok base is 737-4D7 HS-TDG *Kalasin*.

TRANSAVIA AIRLINES
BELOW: Formed in 1965 to operate charters, initially with DC-6s, Transavia soon acquired SE210 Caravelles. They were replaced by Boeing 737s, both the series -200 and -300, and later still 757s. The airline's first scheduled service was Amsterdam–Gatwick, a route now served five times a day. The 737-200s have all been disposed of, but the -300 fleet now totals 12. A single series -400 was acquired on short-term lease early in 1997 and the airline has eight -800s on order. Featuring the airline's current livery at Gatwick is 737-3K2 PH-HVN.

TransBrasil

Top Left: One of Brazil's three international airlines, it operates an all-Boeing fleet of 737s and 767s. The 737 fleet comprising six -300s and four -400s are all leased. The airline's rainbow coloured fin provide a nice contrast to the hills in the background at Santos Dumont airport on 737-3Q4 PT-TEH.

TAP–Air Portugal

Centre Left: Until 1979 Portugal's national airline was known as as TAP (Transportes Aereos Portugueses), on which date it became TAP–Air Portugal. The airline was a late member of the 737 club, not receiving the first of its six -200s until June 1983. The first of eight -300s joined the fleet in March 1989, and these have since been joined by a further two examples previously leased to Air Malta. CS-TIN is one of these latter aircraft, and is here seen on approach to Heathrow.

Bottom Left: Early in 1997 TAP–Air Portugal applied special colour schemes to two of its Boeing 737-300s. One was a mainly pale blue scheme promoting tourism in the Algarve. The other is a somewhat garish multi-coloured scheme to promote

Expo '98 in Lisbon, and is seen here on 737-382 CS-TIB named *Acores* at Berlin/Tegel in May 1997.

Tunisair

Above: The 737 operations of Tunisair somewhat mirror those of Egyptair, with series -200s being acquired from the end of the 1970s, and the first of four -500s from April 1992. The airline's current livery was introduced in 1991, and is seen here on 737-5H3 TS-IOG named after the town *Sfax* as it climbs out of Amsterdam's Schiphol airport.

Turkmenistan Airlines

Below: With the break up of the former Soviet Union a number of the emerging states started forming their own airlines, and many are now acquiring modern western airliners. Turkmenistan Airlines has been more adventurous than most, acquiring three Boeing 737-300s and three 757s. These aircraft now link the capital Ashkhabad with several western cities, including both London and Birmingham in the UK. Photographed at the latter venue is 737-332 EZ-A002. *Paul Sliwinski*

VANGUARD AIRLINES

MAIN PICTURE: A Kansas City-based operator formed in 1994, Vanguard Airlines currently utilises seven series -200s. Two former TransBrasil series -300s were acquired in December 1995, but have recently been passed on to America West Airlines. These aircraft were registered N303AL and N304AL, with the former photographed on approach to Los Angeles.

UNITED AIRLINES

INSET LEFT: United Airlines unveiled its latest livery in January 1993 having successfully managed to keep the news secret until then. Looking immaculate in the new scheme as it approaches Los Angeles is 737-322 N357UA.

USAirways

INSET RIGHT: The mid-1990s have proved to be boom years for the major US airlines — with one or two exceptions. Trans World is still in dire straits and USAir has struggled to reach profitability, despite its code-share deal with and injection of funds from British Airways. This deal is however now 'dead in the water' due to BA's proposed link-up with American Airlines. Whether by design or accident, the British carrier has actually done rather well out of it brief engagement with USAir, as the latter's three transatlantic services to London Gatwick have been taken over by BA. In late 1996 USAir announced a range of improvements in its bid to enhance its image and profits, including a name change to US Airways and a revised livery. I'm sure that it could have come up with something better than the rather drab black and grey scheme seen here on 737-3B4 N522AU at Toronto.

VARIG

ABOVE: Brazil's national carrier operates a large but predominantly Boeing-manufactured fleet of 727s, 737s, 747s and 767s, augmented by a few DC-10s and MD-11s. Varig's 737 fleet still comprises 17 -200s, but also includes 28 -300s with more on order. Early in 1997 the airline introduced a new livery, but it will be some time before it appears on all their aircraft. Featuring the old paint scheme on the taxiway at Rio de Janeiro's Galeao international airport is 737-3K9 PP-VOY.

VASP

BELOW: Sao Paulo-based VASP is the third of Brazil's international carriers. The airline received its first 737 back in July 1969 and currently operates 22 ageing -200s, although six -300s were leased from GPA in 1987 — due to problems with lease payments these aircraft were returned to the lessor in late 1992 and early 1993. The airline currently has a pair of -300s on lease from Maersk Air, and these are used on the 'air bridge' between the compact downtown airports of Sao Paulo/ Congonhas and Rio de Janeiro/Santos Dumont. Seen soon after repossession by GPA and still in its livery, is VASP series -300 PP-SNV which carries the ferry flight registration PT-WBI. The new 747s in the background are being prepared for delivery.

VIRGIN ATLANTIC

TOP RIGHT: The appearance of a 737-400 in Virgin Atlantic colours came as something of a surprise — however its duration was limited to the summer of 1993. The reason was the introduction of an Athens–London service operated by the new Greek carrier South East European Airways in a franchise agreement with Virgin. Air UK Leisure 737-400 G-UKLB was leased as neither airline had suitable equipment to operate the service. This service has, however, since been worked by an A320, and is now operated solely by Virgin as the Greek carrier is no more.

VIRGIN EXPRESS

CENTRE RIGHT: Boeing 737s in the colours of Virgin Express can now be seen at the airports of many of Europe's capital cities, and there is no doubt that the airline has ruffled the feathers of many of the continent's established national carriers. Sabena however adopted the strategy that it was best to work with the newcomer rather than against it, especially as the low cost carrier is also Brussels based. Virgin Express now operates services from Brussels to both Heathrow and Gatwick on behalf of Sabena, with both carriers selling tickets. Seen on approach to Heathrow in Virgin Express's high profile vivid red and white livery is 737-3M8 OO-LTL.

VIVA AIR

BOTTOM RIGHT: Climbing out of Gatwick bound for Palma is 737-3Q8 EC-FER belonging to Viva Air. The airline was formed in 1988 as a subsidiary of Iberia with the aim of capturing a share of the increasing holiday charter market to Spain — particularly to its base at Palma. Viva has only ever operated Boeing 737-300s, nine of which are currently in use. However, Iberia has recently taken back some of the services Viva operated on its behalf and at the time of writing the future of the airline is in doubt, as Iberia has announced that the aircraft of subsidiaries Air Nostrum and Aviaco are to be repainted in Iberia livery.

WESTERN PACIFIC AIRLINES

Founded in 1994, Western Pacific Airlines made an immediate impact on the aviation industry — the reason being the airline's innovative idea for visual style and a novel way of raising revenue. If a company can pay large amounts of money to advertise on television or roadside billboards, then why not on an aircraft? The result is now what is termed 'billboard' schemes, whereby a company will pay the airline for its logo to be painted on an aircraft. An unconfirmed figure of one million dollars has been quoted as the going rate to have your logo painted on an aircraft for one year — and there has been no shortage of customers. Rather surprisingly, apart from Thrifty Rental Cars, no other major national companies have shown an interest. There has, however, been considerable interest from many more local companies, notably hotels, resorts and casinos, but also a television channel advertising its *Simpsons* cartoon series. Western Pacific's fleet of 737-300s currently numbers 19 aircraft with a further two on order. The airline also announced plans to merge with Frontier Airlines, a decision which has since been reversed. In fact on 6 October 1997 Western Pacific filed for Chapter 11 bankruptcy protection after a period of heavy losses which the airline blames on predatory pricing by some of the major US airlines.

LEFT: Advertising the Professional Rodeo Cowboys is 737-3S3 N375TA, which has since been registered N954WP.

BELOW LEFT: The Stardust resort and casino of Las Vegas is obviously doing well, and no doubt have used some of their profits to fund this giant advertising hoarding on former USAir 737-301 N950WP seen here at Phoenix.

ZHONGYUAN AIRLINES

BELOW: Formed in 1986 and based at Zhengzhou, the Chinese independent carrier Zhongyuan Airlines has a fleet of two Yun Y-7s and three Boeing 737-300s. All three 737s were delivered in 1994 and are fitted in a one-class 140-seat configuration. Seen about to line-up on runway 36L at Beijing is 737-37K B-2935.

7 ACCIDENTS

It is true to say that the Boeing 737 has received some unwanted attention due to a number of crashes, however when one considers just how many 737s there are flying around the world today it is inevitable that the type will, from time to time, be the victim of unwarranted and often unfounded criticism. The accident rate of the 737 is certainly no worse, and is much better than most airliner types. This is particularly true of the new generation series -300/-400/-500. Brief details of the few new generation 737s which have been written-off in crashes or suffered serious damage are as follows:

8 January 1989   B737-4Y0 G-OBME East Midlands
G-OBME, British Midland's first series -400 was delivered to the company on 25 October 1988, however a little over two months into its life it met its demise less than a mile from the end of the runway at East Midlands Airport.

The aircraft was some 15 minutes into flight BD092 from London Heathrow to Belfast Aldergrove with eight crew and 117 passengers on board when severe vibration was felt accompanied by a fire warning from the starboard engine. This engine was shut down as per the normal drills and, although the aircraft was between Luton and Birmingham airports the captain elected to divert to the company base at East Midlands /Castle Donington Airport. As the aircraft began its descent the port engine began to lose power.

In the final stages of its approach to runway 27 the aircraft began to loose height, and the crew just managed to clear the village of Kegworth before the tail of the sinking aircraft hit the bank of a cutting on the M1 motorway a mile short of the runway threshold. The aircraft then slid across both carriageways of the normally busy motorway — fortunately during a gap in traffic, and amazingly no vehicles were hit. The aircraft came to rest on the opposite bank, nose high, and the fuselage split into three sections. Fortunately there was no fire but the impact and subsequent injuries resulted in the deaths of 44 on board.

Initial investigations centred on the unheard of failure of both CFM-56-C3 engines. Very soon it became apparent that although the port engine had suffered fire damage, the starboard engine had been functioning properly prior to being shut down after the fire warning. It was then suspected that perhaps crossed wiring may have been a cause, and all series -300 and -400s worldwide were ordered to be checked, but no such faults were found.

Ultimately the investigators came to the conclusion that the pilots had mis-read their instruments and shut down the wrong engine, the perfectly serviceable starboard one. Some crews subsequently complained that the electronic engine instruments were too small and not easy to read. When British Airways ordered the 737-400 it specified anologue engine

instrumention, though it is believed it is the only airline to do so. Several months later there were two further incidents of engine failure concerning the CFM-56-C3, one of which in a strange twist of fate occurred on a British Midland Heathrow–Aldergrove flight! On both occasions the aircraft landed safely.

These incidents prompted the UK Civil Aviation Authority to ground 737s powered by this variant of the CFM-56 engine, a move quickly followed by Boeing. This -3C variant of the CFM-56 was a slightly more powerful variant than the -3B, the additional power being produced by higher rotational speed of the fan. It was determined that the higher speed was causing additional stress, and the reason for the failures.

20 September 1989   B737-401 N416 La Guardia
During the take-off roll during torrential rain at New York's La Guardia Airport, the crew of USAir N416 decided to abort the take-off, presumably because they thought that the aircraft was not going to get airborne on the waterlogged runway. The aircraft however was unable to stop on the runway — no doubt due to aquaplaning — and the Charlotte-bound aircraft slid inexorably into the East River. Unfortunately two of the 61 passengers were killed in the accident.

11 May 1990   B737-3Y0 EI-BZG Manila Airport
During push-back from the terminal at Manila International Airport an explosion on board Philippine Airlines EI-BZG killed eight and injured 30. Initially terrorist action was suspected, however this has been discounted, and it is now thought that vapours in an almost empty centre fuel tank somehow ignited and caused the explosion. At the time of writing this is also thought as the most likely cause of the catastrophic explosion which destroyed the Boeing 747 operating flight TWA800 off New York's Long Island in July 1996.

1 December 19   B737-3B7 N388US Los Angeles Airport
This is one accident which certainly could have been avoided and, fortunately, there were no fatalities aboard the USAir 737. During a night landing at Los Angeles the aircraft landed on top of a Swearingen SA227 Metroliner which had lined-up for departure from an intersection. Reports indicate that initially the 737 crew were unaware of what had actually happened, and that they thought that perhaps the undercarriage had collapsed. Unfortunately there were a number of fatalities aboard the Metroliner.

24 November 1992   B737-3Y0 B-2523 Guilin, China
This aircraft belonging to China Southern was lost when it flew into one of the many spectacular peaks near the popular tourist

ty of Guilin, killing all eight crew and 133 passengers on board. The aircraft was reportedly in a 90° angle of bank at the moment of impact. Some reports suggest that the flight data recorder indicated that the starboard engine suffered severe vibration in the final minutes of the ill-fated flight.

0 March 1993   B737-3Z6 33-333/HS-TGQ Nr Bangkok
This aircraft belonging to the Royal Flight of the Royal Thai Air Force was lost soon after take-off from Bangkok's Don Muang airport during a post maintenance air test, unfortunately all six on board were killed, including a Boeing engineer. The aircraft had undergone maintenance to correct a mis-trimmed horizontal stabilizer, and while in the circuit at Muang Khon Kaen the aircraft suddenly pitched nose up, then quickly nose down. In the ensuing stall the aircraft pancaked and was destroyed.

5 July 1993
B737-5L9 HL7229 Mokpo Airport, South Korea
This particular aircraft was delivered to the Danish airline Maersk Air as OY-MAB, and was one of two subsequently leased to Asiana in November 1992. The aircraft was lost on a VOR/DME approach to Mokpo Airport, South Korea. This was the third such approach to the airport in bad weather conditions when it crashed into high ground seven kilometres from the end of runway, killing three crew and 63 passengers. Three other crew members and 47 passengers survived the accident. This is the only -500 which has been lost to date.

September 1994
B737-3Y0 N513AU Aliquippa, PA. USA
This USAir -300 as flight 427 was *en-route* to Pittsburgh when it suddenly plunged to the ground near Aliquippa, Pennsylvania, killing all 132 passengers and crew on board. At the time the weather was perfect, and whilst in the descent the aircraft was seen by several eyewitnesses to bank to the left before entering a steep dive. The loss of this aircraft, along with a series -200 of United Airlines at Colorado Springs in 1991 are the cause of much concern today because, despite in-depth investigations, no cause can be found for either. There is inevitably however much speculation!

29 December 1994   B737-4Y0 TC-JES Van, Turkey
20 months after delivery, 737-400 TC-JES was written-off in a fatal crash whilst on approach to the airport of the remote city of Van in eastern Turkey. The aircraft belonging to THY was operating flight TK278 from Ankara with 69 passengers and seven crew on board. The captain abandoned the first approach in deteriorating weather conditions of fog and snow, and was about to divert back to Ankara when he decided on another attempt at the VOR/DME approach to runway 03.

During the second approach the aircraft hit a hill 5 miles (8km) from touchdown. This hill is 5,700ft (1,737m) above sea level, however Van airport is 5,470ft (1,667m) above sea level. 52 of the passengers and two of the crew were killed, and under the circumstances it is amazing that 19 people survived.

8 May 1997   B737-31B B-2925 Huanglian, China
This China Southern aircraft was on a flight from Chongqing to Shenzhen, however due to thunderstorms in the vicinity of Shenzhen airport the pilot elected to divert to nearby Huanglian. The first attempted approach in turbulent conditions resulted in a heavy landing, and the pilot selected maximum power and went around for another attempt. During the subsequent landing nine minutes later the aircraft fuselage broke into three sections and caught fire. Of the 74 passengers and nine crew on board, 33 passengers and two crew members, including the first officer, were killed. Reports suggest that during the first attempted landing the nosewheel leg was pushed up into the fuselage and probably weakened the structural integrity of the aircraft.

Incidents Caused By Unexpected Rudder Reversal
The reasons for the loss of the USAir -300 and a United -200 in 1991 have never been ascertained — despite exhaustive investigations by the US National Transportation Safety Board (NTSB). Both aircraft suddenly plunged to the ground out of control. Although investigations are inconclusive, investigators believe that a sudden uncommanded rudder movement put both aircraft out of control and into a dive whilst inbound to their destination airport.

On both occasions the weather was clear, and as the aircraft were in the descent there was almost certainly insufficient altitude and time to enable the crew to recover from the uncommanded input. At slow speed and low altitude a large rudder deflection could make the aircraft difficult to control and induce severe roll. In the summer of 1996 a British Airways 737-200 on an post maintenance air test out of Gatwick suddenly went out of control. The crew skillfully managed to recover the aircraft — fortunately for them they were at a high enough altitude which made the recovery possible — as the aircraft lost some 10,000ft (3,045m) in the process. Had there been a full load of passengers and baggage on board they might not have been so lucky. In June 1996 an Eastwind Airlines 737-200 inbound to Richmond, Virginia, suffered from rudder control problems but, thankfully, the crew were able to make a safe landing.

The NTSB believe that the fault lies in the rudder power control unit (PCU). Tests and a series of special controlled experiments of the PCU from the USAir machine have led them to believe that the servo valve's secondary slide in the main rudder PCU could jam and cause a rudder reversal. This means that the rudder could move in the opposite direction to that demanded by the pilot, and if this is not recognised and acted upon immediately, then control of the aircraft could be lost.

The NTSB urged the US Federal Aviation Administration (FAA) to take two courses of action. Firstly to redesign and install the PCU as soon as possible and, secondly, to train pilots to react and cope with an unexpected rudder reversal. Soon afterwards the FAA also instructed operators of US registered 737s to remove the PCU and check for a cracked bearing. This was the result of a cracked bearing being found in one PCU caused by the fitting of an incorrect bolt.

8 PRODUCTION HISTORY

Because of the sheer number of aircraft involved in the 737 series -300 to -800, information in this production history has had to be kept to an absolute minimum. Listed, therefore, are: the Boeing line number, the type number, the registraton of the first owner other than Boeing (this does not include registration of the aircraft if the order was not taken up (ntu) or cancelled) and, finally, the date of delivery of the aircraft to the owner. This does not mean that the first owners used the aircraft, as since the middle 1980s large fleets of airliners have been and are still currently being purchased from the manufacturer by specialist leasing companies such as the International Lease Finance Corporation (ILFC) Beverly Hills, California.

Many thanks to the Aviation Hobby Shop for the detailed production list on which this listing is based.

The following airline abbreviations have been used:

AA	American Airlines
ABel	Air Belgium
ABer	Air Berlin
AerL	Aer Lingus
Aerom	Aeromaritime
Aflot	Aeroflot
AirA	Air Austral
AirCal	Air California
AirCh	Air China
AirE	Air Europe
AirF	Air France
AirM	Air Malta
AirN	Air Nauru
AlaskA	Alaska Airlines
Aloha	Aloha Airlines
AmWA	America West Airlines
Ansett	Ansett Airlines
AOF	AOF Leasing Ltd
APac	Air Pacific
ArabL	Arab Leasing
AUKL	Air UK Leisure
AusA	Australian Airlines
BA	British Airways
BAHC	Boullioun Aircraft Holding Company
BAS	Boullioun Aviation Services
BFlug	Bavaria Fluggesellschaft
Braa	Braathens SAFE
CAAC	Civil Aviation Admin of China
CAL	Continental Air Lines
CanAI	Canadian Airlines International
CEA	China Eastern Airlines
ChAF	Chilean Air Force
ChinA	China Airlines
ChHA	China Hanian Airlines
ChSA	China Southern Airlines
ChSWA	China SWA
ChXA	China Xiamen Airlines
ChXha	Chine Xinhua Airlines
ChXinA	China Xinjiang Airlines
ChYA	China Yunnan Airlines
CPAir	Canadian Pacific Air Lines
CSA	CSA-Czech Airlines
DANL	DAN Lease Co Ltd
DBA	Deutsche BA
Delta	Delta Air Lines
DML	Dormacken Ltd
DNB	DNB Lease Co Ltd
EasyJ	easyJet Airline Company Ltd
Egyp	Egyptair
EurI	Euralair International
EWA	Eastwind Airlines
FlugHS	Flugzeugvermietsgmbh Hunold-Schulte
Garuda	Garuda Indonesian Airways
GATX	GATX Capital Corporation
GBAir	GB Airways
GECAS	General Electric Capital Aviation Services
GECC	General Electric Capital Corporation
Ger	Germania
GPA	GPA Group Ltd
Hell	Heller Financial
HL	Hapag Lloyd
Ice	Icelandair
ILC	Itochu Lease Company Ltd
ILFC	International Lease Finance Corporation
JAL	Japan Air Lines
Jet	Jet Airways
JTA	Japan Transocean Airlines
JugA	Jugoslovenski Aerotransport
Kenya	Kenya Airways
KLM	KLM-Royal Dutch Airlines
Lauda	Lauda Air
Lflyg	Linjeflyg
LOT	LOT-Polish Airlines
Luft	Lufthansa
MAS	Malaysian Airline System
Malay	Malaysian Airlines
MidAL	Midway Airlines
MskA	Maersk Air
Nippon	Air Nippon
Nord	Nordstress Ltd
Novel	Novel Leasing
NovIA	Novair International Airways
NCA	North China Administration
NSA	NSA Turkmenistan
Olymp	Olympic Airways
Orion	Orion Airways
PAF	Peruvian Air Force
PakIA	Pakistan International Airlines
PemCC	Pembroke Capital Corporation
PHT	Pegasus Hava Tasimaciligi
Pied	Piedmont Airlines
ProA	Pro Air
Qantas	Qantas
RAMar	Royal Air Maroc
RThAF	Royal Thai Air Force
SAB	SABENA
SAS	Scandinavian Airlines System
ShA	Shandong Airlines
ShenA	Shenzen Airlines
SKAF	South Korean Air Force
Sobel	Sobelair
SPEF	Security Pacific Equipment Finance
SunAC	Sunrock Aircraft Corporation
SWA	Southwest Airlines
TAAG	TAAG Angola Airlines
TACA	TACA International Airlines
TEA	TEA Switzerland
TexAC	Texas Air Corporation
Thai	Thai Airways International
THY	THY-Turkish Airlines
TPEL	Trans-Pacific Enterprises Inc
TransA	Transavia Airlines
TransEA	Trans European Airways
TransH	Transavia Holland
TunisA	Tunis Air
UAL	United Airlines
UTA	Union de Transports Aeriens
VASP	VASP Leasing
Virgin	Virgin Express
VIVA	Viva Air
WAL	Western Air Lines
WTC	Wilmington Trust Corp
YunnPA	Yunnan Provincial Aviation
ZhoA	Zhongyuan Airlines

Line No	Type No	First Owner Reg	First Owner	Delivery	Line No	Type No	First Owner Reg	First Owner	Delivery	Line No	Type No	First Owner Reg	First Owner	Delivery
1001	3B7	N350AU	US Air	30.4.85	1106	347	N302WA	WAL	26.4.85	1136	3H9	YU-ANF	JugA	15.8.8
1007	3B7	N351AU	US Air	27.11.85	1107	3Q8	G-SCUH	ILFC	2.5.85	1137	3B7	N358AU	US Air	31.7.8
1015	3B7	N352AU	US Air	11.4.85	1108	347	N303WA	WAL	7.5.85	1138	3H4	N304SW	SWA	22.8.8
1022	3B7	N353AU	US Air	28.11.84	1110	317	C-FCPJ	CP Air	7.5.85	1139	3H4	N305SW	SWA	28.8.8
1030	3B7	N354AU	US Air	5.12.84	1111	3L9	OY-MMK	MskA	24.5.85	1140	3B7	N359AU	US Air	23.8.8
1037	3H4	N300SW	SWA	30.11.84	1112	301	N303P	Pied	20.5.85	1141	3T0	N17306	TexAC	28.8.8
1043	3B7	N355AU	US Air	11.12.84	1114	340	AP-BCA	PakIA	31.5.85	1142	3T0	N14307	TexAC	27.8.8
1048	3H4	N301SW	SWA	20.12.84	1115	301	N304P	Pied	23.5.85	1144	3T0	N14308	TexAC	5.9.8
1052	3H4	N302SW	SWA	20.12.84	1116	340	AP-BCB	PakIA	3.6.85	1145	3B7	N360AU	US Air	13.9.8
1057	3B7	N356AU	US Air	19.12.84	1118	3L9	OY-MML	MskA	10.6.85	1146	301	N309P	Pied	5.9.8
1063	3A4	N307AC	ILFC	1.2.85	1119	3T0	N16301	TexAC	7.6.85	1147	3T0	N17309	TexAC	13.9.8
1069	3T5	G-BLKB	Orion	29.1.85	1121	340	AP-BCC	PakIA	18.6.85	1148	3H4	N306SW	SWA	30.9.8
1073	3Z8	101	SKAF	30.1.85	1122	340	AP-BCD	PakIA	21.6.85	1149	3B7	N361AU	US Air	18.9.8
1076	3G7	N150AW	AmWA	20.2.85	1123	340	AP-BCE	PakIA	25.6.85	1150	3T0	N16310	TexAC	24.9.8
1080	3T5	G-BLKC	Orion	11.3.85	1124	301	N305P	Pied	20.6.85	1152	3T0	N69311	TexAC	30.9.8
1087	347	N3301	WAL	29.3.85	1125	3Q8	N841L	ILFC	26.6.85	1153	3T0	N60312	TexAC	3.10.8
1090	3G7	N151AW	AmWA	13.3.85	1126	301	N306P	Pied	25.6.85	1156	3H4	N307SW	SWA	30.10.8
1092	3T5	G-BLKE	Orion	25.3.85	1127	3B7	N357AU	US Air	28.6.85	1157	301	N312P	Pied	11.10.8
1094	3A4	N308AC	ILFC	1.4.85	1128	3Q8	N871L	ILFC	11.7.85	1158	3T0	N12313	TexAC	16.10.8
1096	3A4	N309AC	ILFC	27.3.85	1129	3T0	N59302	TexAC	19.7.85	1159	3T0	N71314	TexAC	24.10.8
1098	317	C-FCPG	CP Air	12.4.85	1130	3T0	N77303	TexAC	24.7.85	1160	3H4	N309SW	SWA	30.10.8
1100	3A4	N301AC	AirCal	15.5.85	1131	3T0	N61304	TexAC	30.7.85	1161	3H4	N310SW	SWA	20.12.8
1101	3H4	N303SW	SWA	15.4.85	1132	301	N307P	Pied	15.7.85	1162	3B7	N362AU	US Air	8.11.8
1103	301	N301P	Pied	19.4.85	1133	3T0	N63305	TexAC	13.8.85	1163	3Q8	N152AW	ILFC	13.11.8
1104	317	C-FCPI	CP Air	26.4.85	1134	3H9	YU-AND	JugA	31.7.85	1164	301	N313P	Pied	4.12.85

Line No	Type No	First Owner Reg	First Owner	Delivery
166	3W0	B-2517	ChYA	12.12.85
168	3Z0	B-2519	ChSWA	17.12.85
169	301	N314P	Pied	12.12.85
170	347	N304WA	WAL	19.11.85
171	3H9	YU-ANH	JugA	10.12.85
172	347	N305WA	WAL	3.12.85
173	347	N306WA	WAL	6.12.85
174	3T0	N34315	TexAC	27.11.85
175	3H9	YU-ANI	JugA	17.12.85
177	3B7	N363AU	US Air	20.12.85
179	3B7	N364AU	US Air	20.12.85
180	3T0	N17316	TexAC	18.12.85
181	3T0	N17317	TexAC	19.12.85
182	3A4	N303AC	AirCal	19.12.85
183	3H4	N311SW	SWA	13.3.86
184	3Z0	B-2520	ChSWA	25.1.86
185	3H4	N312SW	SWA	14.3.86
187	3Q8	N891L	ILFC	28.1.86
188	3T0	N12318	TexAC	15.1.86
190	3T0	N12319	TexAC	22.1.86
191	3T0	N14320	TexAC	30.1.86
192	3T0	N17321	TexAC	5.2.86
193	3W0	B-2518	ChYA	8.3.86
195	3K2	PH-HVF	TransH	28.2.86
196	3Z0	B-2521	ChSWA	26.2.86
198	3K2	PH-HVG	TransH	17.3.86
200	301	N315P	Pied	4.3.86
201	3H4	N313SW	SWA	17.3.86
202	3T0	N12322	TexAC	27.2.86
204	3T0	N10323	TexAC	10.3.86
205	3A4	N304AC	AirCal	13.3.86
206	3Y0	G-DHSW	GPA	13.3.86
207	3T0	N14324	TexAC	17.3.86
208	301	N316P	Pied	14.3.86

Line No	Type No	First Owner Reg	First Owner	Delivery
1209	3Q8	OO-ILF	ILFC	17.3.86
1210	3B7	N365AU	US Air	24.3.86
1211	3A4	N306AC	AirCal	2.4.86
1212	3B7	N366AU	US Air	31.3.86
1213	317	C-FCPK	CP Air	2.4.86
1214	301	N317P	Pied	3.4.86
1215	3Q8	N153AW	ILFC	8.4.86
1216	317	C-FCPL	CP Air	9.4.86
1217	3Y0	N67AB	GPA	11.4.86
1218	347	N307WA	WAL	16.4.86
1219	301	N319P	Pied	1.5.86
1220	347	N308WA	WAL	22.4.86
1221	3B7	N367AU	US Air	23.4.86
1222	301	N320P	Pied	1.5.86
1224	3J6	B-2531	CAAC	15.5.86
1225	376	VH-TAF	AusA	3.10.86
1227	3Y0	G-MONF	GPA	13.5.86
1228	3T0	N14325	TexAC	19.5.86
1229	3H4	N314SW	SWA	19.5.86
1230	3T0	N17326	TexAC	20.5.86
1231	3H4	N315SW	SWA	30.5.86
1232	3H4	N316SW	SWA	30.5.86
1233	3Y0	G-MONG	GPA	28.5.86
1234	3B7	N368AU	US Air	30.5.86
1235	340	AP-BCF	PakIA	20.6.86
1237	3J6	B-2532	CAAC	19.6.86
1238	3T0	N12327	TexAC	12.6.86
1239	347	N309WA	WAL	13.6.86
1240	3Z0	B-2522	ChSWA	10.7.86
1242	3Y0	PT-TEA	GPA	23.6.86
1243	3Y0	PT-TEB	GPA	25.6.86
1244	3T0	N17328	TexAC	10.7.86
1246	330	D-ABXA	Luft	13.8.86
1247	3T0	N17329	TexAC	15.7.86

Line No	Type No	First Owner Reg	First Owner	Delivery
1248	301	N321P	Pied	9.7.86
1249	3Q8	N781L	ILFC	2.7.86
1250	3B7	N369AU	US Air	17.7.86
1251	376	VH-TAG	AusA	25.7.86
1252	3Q8	N751L	ILFC	18.7.86
1253	3T0	N70330	TexAC	25.7.86
1254	3Z9	OE-FGW	Lauda	ntu
1255	3H4	N318SW	SWA	11.8.86
1258	3T0	N13331	TexAC	11.8.86
1259	376	VH-TAH	AusA	11.8.86
1260	377	VH-CZA	Ansett	22.8.86
1263	3T0	N47332	TexAC	21.8.86
1264	376	VH-TAI	AusA	22.8.86
1268	301	N322P	Pied	3.9.86
1269	347	N2310	WAL	29.8.86
1270	376	VH-TAJ	AusA	5.9.86
1271	330	D-ABXB	Luft	11.9.86
1272	330	D-ABXC	Luft	18.9.86
1273	377	VH-CZB	Ansett	16.9.86
1274	377	VH-CZC	Ansett	25.9.86
1275	306	PH-BDA	KLM	30.9.86
1276	3T0	N69333	TexAC	3.10.86
1277	376	VH-TAK	AusA	3.11.86
1278	330	D-ABXD	Luft	2.10.86
1279	377	VH-CZD	Ansett	9.10.86
1280	377	VH-CZE	Ansett	15.10.86
1281	377	VH-CZF	Ansett	23.10.86
1282	330	D-ABXE	Luft	9.10.86
1283	33A	N164AW	TPEL	2.10.86
1284	33A	N165AW	TPEL	3.10.86

BELOW: Philippines Airlines 737-300 about to depart for Cebu from Hong Kong's Kai Tak International airport.

111

Line No	Type No	First Owner Reg	First Owner	Delivery
1285	330	D-ABXF	Luft	16.10.86
1286	376	VH-TAU	AusA	1.12.86
1287	347	N311WA	WAL	16.10.86
1288	306	PH-BD	KLM	14.10.8
1289	347	N312WA	WAL	29.10.86
1290	330	D-ABXH	Luft	6.11.86
1291	301	N323P	Pied	16.10.86
1292	377	VH-CZG	Ansett	20.11.86
1293	330	D-ABXI	Luft	13.11.86
1294	377	VH-CZH	Ansett	25.11.86
1295	306	PH-BDC	KLM	29.10.86
1296	3T0	N14334	TexAC	30.10.86
1297	330	D-ABXK	Luft	20.11.86
1298	3T0	N14335	TexAC	17.11.86
1300	322	N301UA	UAL	12.11.86
1301	3Q8	EC-EAK	ILFC	10.11.86
1302	33A	N166AW	TPEL	10.11.86
1303	306	PH-BDD	KLM	13.11.86
1304	33A	N167AW	TPEL	13.11.86
1305	3H9	YU-ANJ	JugA	17.11.86
1306	376	VH-TAV	AusA	12.12.86
1307	330	D-ABXL	Luft	4.12.86
1308	3B7	N370AU	USAir	19.11.86
1309	306	PH-BDE	KLM	29.11.86
1310	3H9	YU-ANK	JugA	26.11.86
1311	33A	N168AW	TPEL	1.12.86
1314	377	VH-CZI	Ansett	11.12.86
1315	322	N302UA	UAL	11.12.86
1316	377	VH-CZJ	Ansett	16.12.86
1317	306	PH-BDG	KLM	17.12.86
1318	3A4	N310AC	AirCal	19.12.86
1320	3B7	N371AU	USAir	18.12.86
1321	3H9	YU-ANL	JugA	19.12.86
1322	322	N303UA	UAL	23.12.86
1323	377	VH-CZK	Ansett	8.1.87
1324	347	N313WA	WAL	23.12.86
1325	306	PH-BDH	KLM	15.1.87
1326	377	VH-CZL	Ansett	15.1.87
1327	301	N324P	Pied	13.1.87
1328	3T0	N14336	TexAC	16.1.87
1330	322	N304UA	UAL	23.1.87
1331	301	N325P	Pied	22.1.87
1332	322	N305UA	UAL	27.1.87
1333	3T0	N14337	TexAC	30.1.87
1334	322	N306UA	UAL	30.1.87
1335	306	PH-BDI	KLM	4.2.87
1336	3S3	G-BMTE	AirE	10.2.87
1337	33A	N172AW	TPEL	4.2.87
1338	3T0	N59338	TexAC	12.2.87
1339	3B7	N372AU	USAir	9.2.87
1340	3T0	N16339	TexAC	12.2.87
1341	3S3	G-BMTF	AirE	12.2.87
1343	306	PH-BDK	KLM	4.2.87
1344	33A	N173AW	TPEL	19.2.87
1345	3S3	G-BMTG	AirE	27.2.87
1346	322	N307UA	UAL	26.2.87
1348	3H4	N319SW	SWA	4.3.87
1349	306	PH-BDL	KLM	25.2.87
1350	3H4	N320SW	SWA	6.3.87
1351	3H4	N321SW	SWA	6.3.87
1352	376	VH-TAW	AusA	6.4.87
1353	3Y0	EI-BTF	GPA	11.3.87
1354	322	N308UA	UAL	16.3.87
1355	301	N326P	Pied	13.3.87
1356	376	VH-TAX	AusA	6.4.87
1357	3Y0	G-MONH	GPA	19.3.87
1358	3T0	N39340	TexAC	23.3.87
1359	3S3	G-BMTH	AirE	25.3.87
1360	3K2	PH-HVJ	TransA	26.3.87
1362	3B7	N373AU	USAir	26.3.87
1363	3Y0	EC-EBX	GPA	1.4.87
1364	322	N309UA	UAL	11.4.87
1365	3L9	OY-MMM	MskA	6.4.87
1366	3B7	N374AU	USAir	7.4.87
1367	301	N327P	Pied	8.4.87
1368	3T0	N14341	TexAC	13.4.87
1370	322	N310UA	UAL	16.4.87
1372	3Y0	EI-BTM	GPA	21.4.87
1373	3T0	N14342	TexAC	22.4.87
1374	3S3	EC-ECM	ILFC	24.4.87
1375	3Q8	G-BNCT	ILFC	24.4.87
1376	3T0	N39343	TexAC	30.4.87
1377	3H4	N322SW	SWA	13.5.87
1378	3H4	N323SW	SWA	13.5.87
1380	301	N328P	Pied	6.5.87
1381	3Y0	EC-EBY	GPA	8.5.87
1382	301	N334P	Pied	11.5.87
1383	3T0	N17344	TexAC	13.5.87
1384	3H4	N324SW	SWA	27.5.87
1385	3T0	N17345	TexAC	18.5.87
1386	3K2	PH-HVK	TransA	13.5.87
1388	375	EC-ECS	CanAI	27.5.87
1389	3Y0	EC-ECR	GPA	22.5.87
1390	376	VH-TAY	AusA	22.6.87
1391	376	VH-TAZ	AusA	22.6.87
1393	3S3	EC-ECQ	ILFC	29.5.87
1394	3B7	N375AU	USAir	8.6.87
1395	375	PT-TEC	CanAI	12.6.87
1396	3T0	N14346	TexAC	15.6.87
1398	3H4	N325SW	SWA	25.6.87
1400	3H4	N326SW	SWA	29.6.87
1404	3T0	N14347	TexAC	29.6.87
1406	301	N335P	Pied	30.6.87
1407	3H4	N327SW	SWA	29.6.87
1408	301	N336P	Pied	30.6.87
1409	39A	VR-CCD	ARAVCO	29.7.87
1410	3B7	N376AU	USAir	10.7.87
1411	3T0	N69348	TexAC	15.7.87
1412	329	OO-SBZ	Sobel	17.7.87
1413	3T0	N12349	TexAC	17.7.87
1416	3K9	PP-VNU	BFlug	4.9.87
1417	3G7	N154AW	AmWA	23.7.87
1419	3G7	N155AW	AmWA	24.7.87
1421	33A	N174AW	TPEL	27.8.87
1422	25A	N724ML	MidAL	3.8.87
1423	33A	N175AW	TPEL	28.8.87
1425	3B7	N377AU	USAir	11.8.87
1427	3B7	N378AU	USAir	14.8.87
1428	301	N337P	Pied	14.8.87
1429	3K9	PP-VNV	BFlug	4.9.87
1430	329	OO-SDV	SAB	25.8.87
1431	3Y0	PT-TED	GPA	25.8.87
1432	329	OO-SDW	SAB	26.8.87
1433	330	D-ABXM	Luft	27.8.87
1434	375	PT-TEE	CanAI	2.9.87
1435	301	N340P	Pied	28.8.87
1436	33A	N6069D	TPEL	9.2.8
1437	301	N341P	Pied	4.9.8
1438	33A	EC-135	TPEL	1.3.8
1439	330	D-ABWA	Condor	17.9.8
1440	3B7	N379AU	USAir	14.9.8
1441	329	OO-SDX	SAB	15.9.8
1442	3B7	N380AU	USAir	17.9.8
1443	329	OO-SDY	SAB	18.9.8
1444	33A	G-BNXW	Nord	9.10.8
1445	3S3	G-BNPA	ILFC	1.10.8
1446	33A	PP-VNT	Nord	10.11.8
1447	330	D-ABXN	Luft	1.10.8
1448	3T0	N18350	TexAC	30.9.8
1449	301	N342P	Pied	30.9.8
1450	3B7	N381AU	USAir	5.10.8
1451	301	N348P	Pied	30.9.8
1452	3B7	N382AU	USAir	8.10.8
1454	330	D-ABWB	Condor	22.10.8
1455	3G7	N156AW	AmWA	15.10.8
1457	3G7	N157AW	AmWA	20.10.8
1458	348	EI-BUD	AerL	28.10.8
1459	3G7	N158AW	AmWA	23.10.8
1460	33A	PP-VNX	Nord	10.11.8
1461	3B7	N383AU	USAir	27.10.8
1462	33A	LN-NOS	Nord	21.8
1463	301	N349P	Pied	30.10.8
1464	3B7	N384AU	USAir	3.11.8
1465	330	D-ABWC	Condor	5.11.8
1466	3T0	N69351	TexAC	9.11.8
1468	3T0	N70352	TexAC	9.11.8
1469	301	N350P	Pied	16.11.8
1470	322	N311UA	UAL	18.11.8
1471	33A	G-OBMA	Nord	18.11.8
1472	3T0	N70353	TexAC	19.11.8
1473	33A	G-OBMB	Nord	9.12.8
1474	348	EI-BUE	AerL	25.11.8
1475	3B7	N385AU	USAir	25.11.8
1476	3T0	N76354	TexAC	16.12.8
1477	301	N352P	Pied	2.12.8
1478	3T0	N76355	TexAC	16.12.8
1479	322	N312UA	UAL	7.12.8
1480	3B7	N386AU	USAir	14.12.8
1481	322	N313UA	UAL	8.12.8
1483	322	N314UA	UAL	16.12.8
1484	3A4	N32836	ILFC	22.12.8
1487	401	N404US	Pied	2.3.8
1488	3B7	N387AU	USAir	23.12.8
1489	330	D-ABXO	Luft	7.1.8
1467	35B	D-AGEA	Ger	20.11.8
1482	35B	D-AGEB	Ger	14.12.8
1485	322	N315UA	UAL	23.12.8
1491	322	N316UA	UAL	15.1.8
1494	3G7	N159AW	AmWA	20.1.8
1495	330	D-ABXP	Luft	21.1.8
1496	3G7	N160AW	AmWA	21.1.8
1497	3B7	N388AU	USAir	27.1.8
1498	301	N353P	Pied	26.1.8
1499	3B7	N389AU	USAir	1.2.8
1500	330	D-ABXR	Luft	4.2.8
1501	3B7	N390AU	USAir	10.2.8
1503	3B7	N391AU	USAir	14.3.8
1504	322	N318UA	UAL	9.2.8
1505	3T0	N75356	TexAC	2.3.8

Line No	Type No	First Owner Reg	First Owner	Delivery	Line No	Type No	First Owner Reg	First Owner	Delivery	Line No	Type No	First Owner Reg	First Owner	Delivery
506	3Q8	G-BNNJ	ILFC	11.2.88	1545	3H4	N332SW	SWA	9.5.88	1591	3H4	N339SW	SWA	24.8.88
507	3T0	N19357	TexAC	2.3.88	1546	322	N321UA	UAL	6.5.88	1593	3H4	N341SW	SWA	24.8.88
508	330	D-ABWD	Condor	18.2.88	1547	3H4	N333SW	SWA	12.5.88	1595	33A	F-GFUC	Nord	23.8.88
509	3B7	N392AU	USAir	13.4.88	1548	322	N322UA	UAL	11.5.88	1596	401	N411US	Pied	19.10 .88
510	301	N355P	Pied	19.2.88	1549	3H4	N334SW	SWA	22.5.88	1597	33A	F-GFUD	Nord	14.9.88
511	3Y0	PT-TEI	GPA	25.2.88	1550	322	N323UA	UAL	17.5.88	1598	3Q8	EC-189	ILFC	1.11.88;
512	401	N405US	Pied	28.2.89	1551	3B7	N393AU	USAir	16.5.88	1599	33A	G-MONP	Nord	5.10.88
513	3Y0	EI-BTT	GPA	26.2.88	1552	301	N358P	Pied	18.5.88	1601	33A	G-MONN	Nord	5.10.88
514	330	D-ABWE	Condor	7.3.88	1553	3H4	N335SW	SWA	27.5.88	1603	4Y0	G-OBME	GPA	25.10.88
515	3Z9	OE-ILG	Lauda	2.3.88	1554	301	N359P	Pied	24.5.88	1606	3G7	N303AW	AmWA	13.9.88
516	3T0	N27358	TexAC	10.3.88	1556	33A	F-GFUB	Nord	1.6.88	1608	3G7	N304AW	AmWA	6.10.88
517	3S3	G-BNPB	AirE	7.3.88	1557	3H4	N336SW	SWA	31.5.88	1610	401	N412US	Pied	31.10 .88
518	3T0	N18359	TexAC	15.3.88	1558	3T0	N76362	TexAC	3.6.88	1612	3G7	N305AW	AmWA	11.10.88
519	3S3	G-BNPC	AirE	9.3.88	1559	301	N588US	Pied	2.6.88	1614	3M8	OO-LTA	TransEA	3.10.88
520	3T0	N76360	TexAC	21.3.88;	1560	3B7	N394AU	USAir	6.6.88	1616	4Y0	G-OBMF	GPA	4.11.88
521	3H4	N328SW	SWA	24.3.88	1561	401	N408US	Pied	27.9.88	1618	377	VH-CZM	Ansett	11.10.88
522	3T0	N76361	TexAC	31.3.88	1562	3Y0	PT-TEJ	GPA	1.7.88	1620	377	VH-CZN	Ansett	12.10.88
525	3H4	N329SW	SWA	28.3.88	1563	301	N589US	Pied	10.6.88	1621	401	N413US	Pied	14.11 .88
527	3T5	G-BNRT	Orion	28.3.88	1564	322	N324UA	UAL	16.6.88	1622	377	VH-CZO	Ansett	18.10.88
528	401	N406US	Pied	15.9.88	1566	322	N325UA	UAL	21.6.88	1630	3M8	OO-LTB	TransEA	7.11.88
529	3H4	N330SW	SWA	29.3.88	1567	3H4	N337SW	SWA	30.6.88	1631	401	N415US	Pied	22.11.88
531	3G7	N161AW	AmWA	4.4.88	1568	322	N326UA	UAL	23.6.88	1635	4Q8	G-BNNK	ILFC	30.11.88
532	322	N319UA	UAL	12.4.88	1569	301	N590US	Pied	1.7.88	1637	341	PP-VOD	VARIG	29.11.88
533	3G7	N162AW	AmWA	7.4.88	1571	3H4	N338SW	SWA	30.6.88	1639	4Y0	HL7251	GPA	5.12.88
534	322	N320UA	UAL	18.4.88	1573	401	N409US	Pied	28.9.88	1641	377	VH-CZP	Ansett	28.11.88
535	3G7	N163AW	AmWA	12.4.88	1575	301	N591US	Pied	7.7.88	1643	401	N416US	Pied	23.12 .88
536	3H4	N331SW	SWA	25.4.88	1576	3G7	N301AW	AmWA	11.7.88	1645	341	PP-VOE	VARIG	7.12.88
537	35B	D-AGEC	Ger	14.4.88	1578	3G7	N302AW	AmWA	15.7.88	1647	4Y0	N1791B	GPA	31.3.89
538	3Y0	EC-151	GPA	20.4.88	1580	3Y0	PT-TEK	GPA	19.7.88	1649	376	VH-TJA	AusA	15.12.88
539	301	N357P	Pied	20.4.88	1582	4Y0	G-UKLA	GPA	14.10.88	1651	4Y0	HL7252	GPA	21.12.88
540	3Y0	EC-152	GPA	22.4.88	1584	3B7	N395AU	USAir	27.7.88	1652	322	N350UA	UAL	31.1.89
542	3Y0	G-BNGL	GPA	26.4.88	1586	3B7	N396AU	USAir	2.8.88					
543	401	N407US	Pied	21.9.88	1587	301	N592US	Pied	2.8.88					
544	3Y0	G-BNGM	GPA	3.5.88	1589	4Y0	TC-ADA	GPA	25.10.88					

BELOW: About to land at Kai Tak is China Southern 737-31B B-2929.

Line No	Type No	First Owner Reg	First Owner	Delivery	Line No	Type No	First Owner Reg	First Owner	Delivery	Line No	Type No	First Owner Reg	First Owner	Delivery
1653	376	VH-TJB	AusA	21.12.88	1724	322	N358UA	UAL	31.5.89	1789	4B7	N426US	USAir	20.10.8
1654	33A	G-OBMC	Nord	9.1.89	1725	3B3	F-GFUF	Aerom	2.6.89	1790	3H4	N351SW	SWA	9.11.8
1655	4Y0	HL7253	GPA	5.1.89	1727	33A	G-PATE	Nord	8.6.89	1791	4B7	N427US	USAir	14.11.8
1656	330	D-ABXS	Luft	12.1.89	1728	322	N359UA	UAL	9.6.89	1792	505	LN-BRC	Braa	7.3.9
1657	382	CS-TIA	ILFC	12.1.89	1729	33A	F-ODGX	Nord	12.6.89	1793	4B7	N428US	USAir	7.12.8
1658	341	PP-VOF	VARIG	12.1.89	1730	322	N360UA	UAL	20.6.89	1794	3K9	CS-TIG	BFlug	7.12.8
1659	4Y0	HL7254	GPA	12.1.89	1731	4Y0	EC-308	GPA	23.6.89	1795	4B7	N429US	USAir	8.12.8
1660	341	PP-VOG	VARIG	17.1.89	1732	401	N423US	Pied	19.6.89	1796	3K9	CS-TIH	BFlug	12.12.8
1661	4Y0	EC-239	GPA	18.1.89	1733	4Y0	PT-TEL	GPA	23.6.89	1797	4B7	N430US	USAir	14.12.8
1662	3M8	OO-LTC	Slibail	19.1.89	1734	3H4	N349SW	SWA	23.6.89	1798	322	N375UA	UAL	18.12.8
1664	330	D-ABXT	Luft	26.1.89	1735	3B7	N530AU	USAir	26.6.89	1799	4B7	N431US	USAir	22.12.8
1665	4Q8	G-BNNL	ILFC	26.1.89	1736	4S3	G-BPKE	AirE	30.6.89	1800	3L9	OY-MME	MskA	17.1.9
1666	3Q8	G-KKUH	ILFC	31.1.89	1737	33A	N731XL	Nord	29.6.89	1801	330	D-ABXY	Luft	11.1.9
1667	4Y0	HL7255	GPA	28.1.89	1739	33A	PP-SNW	Ansett	3.7.89	1802	322	N376UA	UAL	17.1.9
1668	322	N351UA	UAL	9.2.89	1740	376	VH-TJC	AusA	12.7.89	1803	4Y0	HL7260	GPA	16.1.9
1669	33A	G-OBMD	Nord	10.2.89	1741	33A	PP-SNZ	Ansett	6.7.89	1804	5H4	N504SW	SWA	5.3.9
1670	322	N352UA	UAL	9.2.89	1742	448	EI-BXA	AerL	12.7.89	1805	4Y0	EC-401	GPA	2.2.9
1671	330	ABXU	Luft	9.2.89	1743	3B7	N531AU	USAir	11.7.89	1806	322	N377UA	UAL	24.1.9
1672	322	N353UA	UAL	14.2.89	1744	5H4	N502SW	SWA	7.5.90	1807	330	D-ABXZ	Luft	25.1.9
1673	341	PP-VOH	VARIG	13.2.89	1745	3B7	N532AU	USAir	17.7.89	1808	3Q8	PK-GWE	ILFC	24.1.9
1674	401	N417US	Pied	15.2.89	1746	401	N424US	Pied	18.7.89	1809	3G7	N306AW	AmWA	26.1.9
1675	3M8	HB-IIA	TransEA	13.3.89	1747	4Y0	G-UKLE	GPA	19.7.89	1810	322	N378UA	UAL	30.1.9
1676	401	N418US	Pied	17.2.89	1748	3H4	N350SW	SWA	10.8.89	1811	3Y0	EI-BZH	GPA	30.1.9
1677	330	D-ABWF	Condor	23.2.89	1749	4Y0	HL7257	GPA	25.7.89	1812	322	N379UA	UAL	5.2.9
1678	4Y0	EC-251	GPA	25.2.89	1750	322	N361UA	UAL	28.7.89	1813	3Y0	EI-BZI	GPA	7.2.9
1680	4Y0	HL7256	GPA	28.2.89	1751	4Y0	HL7258	GPA	28.7.89	1814	322	N380UA	UAL	9.2.9
1681	306	PH-BDP	KLM	7.3.89	1752	322	N362UA	UAL	31.7.89	1815	3L9	OY-MMF	MskA	13.2.9
1684	401	N419US	Pied	7.3.89	1753	3Y0	EI-BZE	GPA	2.8.89	1816	5L9	OY-MAA	MskA	6.4.9
1685	330	D-ABWH	Condor	9.3.89	1754	322	N363UA	UAL	4.8.89	1817	4B7	N432US	USAir	14.2.9
1689	3M8	HB-IIB	TransEA	23.3.89	1755	3Y0	EI-BZF	GPA	7.8.89	1818	330	D-ABEA	Luft	20.2.9
1690	3H4	N346SW	SWA	27.3.89	1756	322	N364UA	UAL	10.8.89	1819	4B7	N433US	USAir	20.2.9
1692	322	N354UA	UAL	3.4.89	1757	4Y0	HL7259	GPA	9.8.89	1820	476	VH-TJE	AusA	27.2.9
1693	3B3	F-GFUE	Aerom	1.4.89	1758	322	N365UA	UAL	14.8.89	1821	4B7	N434US	USAir	23.2.9
1694	322	N355UA	UAL	5.4.89	1759	4Y0	PT-TEM	GPA	14.8.89	1822	322	N381UA	UAL	27.2.9
1695	382	CS-TIB	ILFC	30.3.89	1760	322	N366UA	UAL	1.9.89	1823	3G7	N307AW	AmWA	27.2.9
1696	322	N356UA	UAL	5.4.89	1761	376	VH-TJD	AusA	29.8.89	1824	4Y0	9M-MJK	GPA	5.3.9
1698	401	N420US	Pied	5.4.89	1762	322	N367UA	UAL	1.9.89	1825	3G7	N308AW	AmWA	2.3.9
1699	382	CS-TIC	ILFC	6.4.89	1763	33A	G-IEAA	Ansett	18.9.89	1826	5H4	N505SW	SWA	3.4.9
1700	4S3	G-BPKA	AirE	14.4.89	1764	401	N425US	USAir	25.8.89	1827	4K5	D-AHLQ	HL	9.3.9
1691	3Y0	EC-244	GPA	28.4.89	1765	3Q8	PK-GWD	ILFC	28.8.89	1828	4Q8	9M-MJA	ILFC	10.3.9
1701	3Y0	EC-245	GPA	28.4.89	1766	5H4	N503SW	SWA	28.2.90	1829	3Y0	TC-SUN	GPA	13.3.9
1702	4S3	G-BPKB	AirE	14.4.89	1767	3B7	N533AU	USAir	1.9.89	1830	322	N382UA	UAL	19.3.9
1703	3B7	N528AU	USAir	17.4.89	1768	406	PH-BDR	KLM	6.9.89	1831	33A	G-OBMH	Ansett	19.3.9
1704	322	N357UA	UAL	1.5.89	1769	3B7	N534AU	USAir	1.9.89	1832	322	N383UA	UAL	20.3.9
1705	408	TF-FIA	Ice	28.4.89	1770	406	PH-BDS	KLM	23.9.89	1833	33A	G-OBMJ	Ansett	22.3.9
1706	3Q8	PK-GWA	ILFC	24.4.89	1771	3Y0	EI-BZG	GPA	2.10.89	1834	59D	SE-DNA	GPA	10.4.9
1707	4K5	D-AHLL	HL	26.4.89	1772	406	PH-BDT	KLM	28.9.89	1835	4B7	N435US	USAir	26.3.9
1708	3H4	N347SW	SWA	10.5.89	1773	3Z6	HS-TGQ	RThAF	15.9.89	1836	322	N384UA	UAL	28.3.9
1709	329	OO-SYA	SAB	28.4.89	1774	322	N368UA	UAL	20.9.89	1837	3Y0	EI-BZJ	GPA	29.3.9
1710	3H4	N348SW	SWA	12.5.89	1775	3L9	OY-MMD	MskA	18.9.89	1838	322	N385UA	UAL	2.4.9
1711	329	OO-SYB	SAB	2.5.89	1776	322	N369UA	UAL	3.10.89	1839	4K5	N11AB	GPA	5.4.9
1712	3K2	PH-HVN	TransA	4.5.89	1777	4Y0	VR-CAL	GPA	21.9.89	1840	322	N386UA	UAL	5.4.9
1713	3B7	N529AU	USAir	9.5.89	1778	322	N370UA	UAL	2.10.89	1841	4Y0	TC-AFK	GPA	9.4.9
1714	401	N421US	Pied	11.5.89	1779	4Y0	PT-TEN	GPA	10.10.89	1842	505	LN-BRD	Braa	19.4.9
1715	4K5	D-AHLO	HL	11.5.89	1780	322	N371UA	UAL	3.10.89	1843	3G7	N309AW	AmWA	27.3.9
1716	401	N422US	Pied	12.5.89	1781	4Y0	VR-CAB	GPA	2.10.89	1844	46B	0G-BROC	NovIA	12.4.9
1717	3M8	OO-LTD	TransEA	12.5.89	1782	322	N372UA	UAL	27.10.89	1845	4B7	N436US	USAir	16.4.9
1718	5H4	N501SW	SWA	7.9.90	1783	4K5	D-AHLP	HL	18.10.89	1846	3Q8	PK-GWF	ILFC	18.4.9
1719	3M8	OO-LTE	TransEA	18.5.89	1784	322	N373UA	UAL	10.11.89	1847	4B7	N437US	USAir	19.4.9
1720	4S3	G-BPKC	AirE	23.5.89	1785	330	D-ABXW	Luft	24.10.89	1848	5K5	D-AHLE	HL	4.5.9
1721	408	TF-FIB	Ice	23.5.89	1786	322	N374UA	UAL	30.11.89	1849	4B7	N438US	USAir	24.4.9
1722	4S3	G-BPKD	AirE	26.5.89	1787	330	D-ABXX	Luft	24.10.89	1850	448	EI-BXC	AerL	26.4.9
1723	4Y0	G-UKLB	GPA	25.5.89	1788	448	EI-BXB	AerL	27.10.89	1851	408	TF-FIC	Ice	25.4.9

Line No	Type No	First Owner Reg	First Owner	Delivery	Line No	Type No	First Owner Reg	First Owner	Delivery	Line No	Type No	First Owner Reg	First Owner	Delivery
852	5H4	N506SW	SWA	2.5.90	1887	4S3	G-BRKG	AirE	12.7.90	1921	53A	F-GHXM	Ansett	26.9.90
853	3Y0	EI-BZK	GPA	4.5.90	1888	4B6	CN-RMG	RAMar	16.7.90	1922	4D7	HS-TDB	Thai	27.9.90
854	4K5	D-AHLR	HL	4.5.90	1889	322	N390UA	UAL	17.7.90	1923	505	LN-BRG	Braa	28.9.90
855	4Q8	9M-MJB	ILFC	25.4.90	1890	4B6	N440US	USAir	18.7.90	1924	3Q8	PK-GWH	ILFC	28.9.90
856	3K2	PH-HVT	TransA	3.5.90	1891	322	N391UA	UAL	23.7.90	1925	505	LN-BRH	Braa	8.10.90
857	382	CS-TID	ILFC	25.4.90	1892	4B6	N441US	USAir	23.7.90	1926	3K9	PP-VNZ	BFlug	2.10.90
858	3K2	PH-HVV	TransA	11.5.90	1893	322	N392UA	UAL	26.7.90	1927	3Y0	EI-BZL	GPA	4.10.90
859	4Y0	EC-402	GPA	15.5.90	1894	53C	F-GHOL	EurI	27.7.90	1928	322	N399UA	UAL	9.10.90
860	405	LN-BRE	Braa	18.5.90	1895	3M8	F-GKTB	TransEA	27.7.90	1929	3Y0	EI-BZM	GPA	15.10.90
861	4Y0	9M-MJH	GPA	18.5.90	1896	3S1	N371TA	TACA	31.7.90	1930	322	N201UA	UAL	12.10.90
862	322	N387UA	UAL	22.5.90	1897	3Y0	9V-TRA	GPA	30.7.90	1931	4B7	N446US	USAir	12.10.90
863	476	VH-TJF	AusA	4.6.90	1898	53A	HL7261	Ansett	2.8.90	1932	5H4	N508SW	SWA	17.10.90
864	5H4	N507SW	SWA	30.5.90	1899	4D7	HS-TDA	Thai	9.8.90	1933	530	D-ABIA	Luft	20.12.90
865	4Y0	TC-ATA	GPA	25.5.90	1900	53A	HL7262	Ansett	7.8.90	1934	5H4	N509SW	SWA	16.10.90
866	4Q8	G-BPNZ	ILFC	30.5.90	1901	4Y0	HR-SHL	GPA	7.8.90	1935	341	PP-VON	VARIG	1.11.90
867	448	EI-BXD	AerL	1.6.90	1902	406	PH-BDU	KLM	14.8.90	1936	4B7	N447US	USAir	23.10.90
868	53A	SE-DNC	Ansett	7.6.90	1903	406	PH-BDW	KLM	21.8.90	1937	322	N202UA	UAL	25.10.90
869	3G7	N311AW	AmWA	7.6.90	1904	4Y0	HR-SHK	GPA	9.8.90	1938	405	LN-BRI	Braa	24.10.90
870	4S3	G-BRKF	AirE	11.6.90	1905	322	N393UA	UAL	14.8.90	1939	548	EI-BXE	AerL	30.10.90
872	59D	SE-DNB	GPA	14.6.90	1906	4B7	N442US	USAir	15.8.90	1940	5H4	N510SW	SWA	30.10.90
873	382	CS-TIE	ILFC	13.6.90	1907	322	N394UA	UAL	20.8.90	1941	3Y0	EI-BZN	GPA	30.10.90
874	4B7	N439US	USAir	18.6.90	1908	4B7	N443US	USAir	20.8.90	1942	3H4	N352SW	SWA	6.11.90
875	322	N388UA	UAL	25.6.90	1909	322	N395UA	UAL	21.8.90	1943	53A	F-GHXN	Ansett	6.11.90
876	4Y0	9M-MJI	GPA	22.6.90	1911	3S1	N372TA	TACA	25.9.90	1944	4B7	N448US	USAir	6.11.90
877	322	N389UA	UAL	26.6.90	1912	476	VH-TJI	AusA	18.9.90	1945	53A	LZ-BOA	Ansett	7.11.90
878	5L9	OY-MAB	MskA	26.6.90	1913	322	N396UA	UAL	12.9.90	1946	4B7	N449US	USAir	9.11.90
879	476	VH-TJG	AusA	3.7.90	1914	4B7	N445US	USAir	13.9.90	1947	3H4	N353SW	SWA	9.11.90
880	4B6	CN-RMF	RAMar	3.7.90	1915	322	N397UA	UAL	14.9.90	1948	522	N901UA	UAL	27.11.90
881	476	VH-TJH	AusA	10.7.90	1916	4B3	F-GFUG	UTA	21.9.90	1949	406	PH-BDY	KLM	17.11.90
882	53A	F-GGML	Ansett	13.7.90	1917	505	LN-BRF	Braa	18.9.90	1950	522	N902UA	UAL	16.11.90
883	4Y0	EC-403	GPA	3.7.90	1917	505	LN-BRM	Braa	26.6.91					
884	3M8	F-GKTA	TransEA	6.7.90	1918	3K9	PP-VNY	BFlug	20.9.90					
885	4Y0	TC-AFL	GPA	10.7.90	1919	5L9	OY-MAC	MskA	20.9.90					
886	3Q8	PK-GWG	ILFC	11.7.90	1920	322	N398UA	UAL	24.9.90					

BELOW: USAir-3B7 N388US climbs out of Toronto on 28 May 1989. 18 months later this aircraft was lost during a night landing at Los Angeles.

Line No	Type No	First Owner Reg	First Owner	Delivery	Line No	Type No	First Owner Reg	First Owner	Delivery	Line No	Type No	First Owner Reg	First Owner	Delivery
1951	341	PP-VOO	VARIG	19.11.90	1982	4B7	N778AU	USAir	22.1.91	2016	3J6	B-2536	AirCh	22.3.9
1952	522	N903UA	UAL	20.11.90	1983	522	N907UA	UAL	23.1.91	2017	3M8	OO-LTK	TransEA	22.3.9
1953	33A	F-GFUI	Ansett	14.12.90	1984	33A	PP-SOD	Ansett	7.2.91	2018	505	D-ACBC	Braa	28.3.9
1954	4B7	N775AU	USAir	29.11.90	1985	530	D-ABIF	Luft	29.1.91	2019	566	SU-GBH	Egyp	10.4.9
1955	33A	PP-SOC	Ansett	11.2.91	1986	4B7	N779AU	USAir	28.1.91	2020	4B7	N784AU	USAir	3.4.9
1956	4B7	N776AU	USAir	29.11.90	1987	522	N908UA	UAL	11.2.91	2021	3Y0	HA-LED	GPA	1.4.9
1957	3Q8	PK-GWI	ILFC	30.11.90	1988	4Y0	TC-JDE	GPA	7.2.91	2022	5K5	D-AHLI	HL	3.4.9
1958	530	D-ABIB	Luft	18.12.90	1989	548	EI-BXH	AerL	4.2.91	2023	530	D-ABIN	Luft	4.4.9
1959	476	VH-TJJ	AusA	11.12.90	1990	4B7	N780AU	USAir	7.2.91	2024	3M8	OO-LTL	TransEA	5.4.9
1960	5Y0	B-2541	GPA	14.1.91	1991	3M8	OO-LTF	TransEA	7.2.91	2025	33A	G-MONV	Ansett	5.4.9
1961	5L9	OY-MAD	MskA	7.12.90	1992	4B7	N781AU	USAir	4.2.91	2026	4B7	N785AU	USAir	9.4.9
1962	53A	LZ-BOB	Ansett	12.12.90	1993	530	D-ABIH	Luft	12.2.91	2027	3Z0	B-2537	ChSWA	12.4.9
1963	4Y0	EI-CBT	GPA	18.12.90	1994	3Q8	PK-GWJ	ILFC	11.2.91	2028	59D	SE-DNE	Lflyg	15.4.9
1964	53A	CN-RMU	Ansett	14.12.90	1995	4B7	N782AU	USAir	14.2.91	2029	5H4	N511SW	SWA	12.4.9
1965	522	N904UA	UAL	14.12.90	1996	4Q8	9M-MJD	ILFC	15.2.91	2030	3Y0	TC-SUR	GPA	18.4.9
1966	5K5	D-AHLD	HL	15.12.90	1997	530	D-ABII	Luft	25.2.91	2031	530	D-ABIO	Luft	18.4.9
1967	530	D-ABIC	Luft	20.12.90	1998	476	VH-TJK	AusA	26.2.91	2033	4Y0	PP-SOJ	GPA	25.4.9
1968	5K5	D-AHLF	HL	18.12.90	1999	522	N909UA	UAL	21.2.91	2034	530	D-ABIP	Luft	30.4.9
1969	59D	SE-DND	Lflyg	21.12.90	2000	530	D-ABIK	Luft	25.2.91	2035	505	LN-BRK	Braa	26.4.9
1970	548	EI-BXF	AerL	19.12.90	2001	3Y0	EI-CBP	GPA	26.2.91	2036	448	EI-BXI	AerL	29.4.9
1971	4Q8	9M-MJC	ILFC	21.12.90	2002	3J6	B-2535	AirCh	13.3.91	2037	3M8	OO-LTM	TransEA	21.5.9
1972	4Y0	9M-MJM	GPA	8.1.91	2003	5Y0	B-2542	GPA	27.2.91	2038	5L9	OY-MAE	MskA	17.5.9
1973	3Y0	9V-TRB	GPA	7.1.91	2004	3M8	OO-XTG	TransEA	28.2.91	2039	3M8	OO-LTN	TransEA	29.5.9
1974	530	D-ABID	Luft	9.1.91	2005	3M8	N760BE	SPEF	17.9.91	2040	3W0	B-2538	YunnPA	8.5.9
1975	548	EI-BXG	AerL	10.1.91	2006	530	D-ABIL	Luft	7.3.91	2041	53C	F-GHUL	EurI	3.5.9
1976	522	N905UA	UAL	15.1.91	2007	3M8	OO-LTJ	TransEA	15.3.91	2042	530	D-ABIR	Luft	3.5.9
1977	53A	N778YY	Ansett	26.6.92	2008	33A	PP-SOE	Ansett	7.3.91	2044	5K5	D-AHLN	HL	9.5.9
1978	4Y0	9M-MJN	GPA	17.1.91	2009	4Y0	9M-MJO	GPA	12.3.91	2045	33A	7Q-YKP	Ansett	20.5.9
1979	530	D-ABIE	Luft	17.1.91	2010	4B7	N783AU	USAir	27.3.91	2046	33A	PP-SOK	Ansett	20.6.9
1980	4B7	N777AU	USAir	18.1.91	2011	530	D-ABIM	Luft	14.3.91	2047	38B	N4320B	SPEF	20.5.9
1981	522	N906UA	UAL	22.1.91	2012	33A	PP-SOF	Ansett	10.4.91	2048	530	D-ABIS	Luft	16.5.9
					2013	3Y0	EI-CBQ	GPA	15.3.91	2049	530	D-ABIT	Luft	23.5.9
					2014	33A	PP-SOG	Ansett	10.4.91	2051	530	D-ABIU	Luft	23.5.9
					2015	3Y0	TC-SUP	GPA	19.3.91	2052	3Y0	B-2523	GPA	23.5.9

BELOW: 737-4Y0 G-OBMF is still in service with British Midland today.

Line No	Type No	First Owner Reg	First Owner	Delivery
2053	35B	D-AGEF	Ger	24.5.91
2054	3Y0	HA-LEF	GPA	24.5.91
2055	4Y0	9M-MJP	GPA	30.5.91
2056	5H4	N512SW	SWA	31.5.91
2057	4Q8	9M-MJE	ILFC	5.6.91
2058	5H4	N513SW	SWA	5.6.91
2059	3L9	OY-MMW	MskA	7.6.91
2060	42C	G-UKLD	AUKL	7.6.91
2061	4S3	N4249R	AOF	11.6.91
2062	42C	G-UKLF	AUKL	11.6.91
2063	530	D-ABIW	Luft	13.6.91
2064	4Y0	9M-MJQ	GPA	14.6.91
2065	33A	F-GFUJ	Ansett	14.6.91
2066	3Y0	HA-LEG	GPA	14.6.91
2067	33A	SE-DPA	Ansett	18.6.91
2068	36E	EC-703	VIVA	27.6.91
2069	33A	PP-SOL	Ansett	20.6.91
2070	530	D-ABIX	Luft	27.6.91
2071	4Y0	TC-JDF	GPA	24.6.91
2073	522	N910UA	UAL	26.6.91
2074	3L9	OY-MMY	MskA	27.6.91
2075	522	N911UA	UAL	28.6.91
2076	4Q8	9M-MJF	ILFC	2.7.91
2077	330	D-ABEB	Luft	3.7.91
2078	5H4	N514SW	SWA	2.7.91
2079	5Y0	B-2543	GPA	3.7.91
2080	5H4	N515SW	SWA	5.7.91
2081	330	D-ABEC	Luft	9.7.91
2082	330	D-ABED	Luft	12.7.91
2083	4S3	9M-MLH	ILFC	20.8.91
2084	330	D-ABEE	Luft	18.7.91
2085	341	PP-VOS	VARIG	23.7.91
2086	530	D-ABIY	Luft	18.7.91
2087	3Y0	B-2525	GPA	17.7.91
2088	46B	OO-ILJ	ABel	17.7.91
2089	3Y0	B-2526	GPA	19.7.91
2090	3K9	PP-VOY	BFlug	19.7.91
2091	341	PP-VOT	VARIG	23.7.91
2092	3H4	N354SW	SWA	23.7.91
2093	5Y0	B-2544	GPA	2.8.91
2094	330	D-ABEF	Luft	31.7.91
2095	5Y0	B-2545	GPA	7.8.91
2096	522	N912UA	UAL	31.7.91
2097	3Y0	B-2527	GPA	9.8.91
2098	530	D-ABIZ	Luft	8.8.91
2100	3K9	PP-VOZ	BFlug	6.8.91
2101	522	N913UA	UAL	6.8.91
2102	330	D-ABEH	Luft	15.8.91
2103	3H4	N355SW	SWA	6.8.91
2104	429	OO-SYC	SAB	13.8.91
2105	3H4	N356SW	SWA	9.8.91
2106	429	OO-SYD	SAB	26.8.91
2107	4B3	F-GFUH	UTA	28.8.91
2108	528	F-GJNB	AirF	28.8.91
2109	484	SX-BKA	Olymp	12.9.91
2110	522	N914UA	UAL	3.9.91
2111	529	OO-SYE	SAB	4.9.91
2112	3G7	N322AW	AmWA	19.9.91
2113	4D7	HS-TDC	Thai	10.9.91
2114	5Q8	SE-DNF	ILFC	11.9.91
2115	4Q8	9M-MJG	ILFC	12.9.91
2116	530	D-ABJA	Luft	6.9.91
2117	530	D-ABJB	Luft	12.9.91
2118	530	D-ABJC	Luft	19.9.91
2119	522	N915UA	UAL	16.9.91
2120	429	OO-SYF	SAB	13.9.91
2121	5H4	N519SW	SWA	17.9.91
2122	530	D-ABJD	Luft	23.9.91
2123	36E	EC-704	VIVA	20.9.91
2124	484	SX-BKB	Olymp	20.9.91
2125	341	PP-VOU	VARIG	11.12.91
2126	530	D-ABJE	Luft	27.9.91
2127	341	PP-VOV	VARIG	11.12.91
2128	530	D-ABJF	Luft	3.10.91
2129	5Q8	SE-DNG	ILFC	30.9.91
2130	484	SX-BKC	Olymp	30.9.91
2131	436	G-DOCA	BA	21.10.91
2132	406	PH-BDZ	KLM	10.10.91
2133	3Q8	PP-VOW	ILFC	4.10.91
2134	5H4	N520SW	SWA	7.10.91
2135	566	SU-GBI	Egyp	11.10.91
2136	5H4	N521SW	SWA	4.10.91
2137	405	LN-BRP	Braa	9.10.91
2138	505	LN-BRN	Braa	10.10.91
2139	3Q8	PP-VOX	ILFC	31.10.91
2140	3L9	OY-MMZ	MskA	16.10.91
2141	530	D-ABJH	Luft	17.10.91
2142	484	SX-BKD	Olymp	17.10.91
2143	505	LN-BRO	Braa	17.10.91
2144	436	G-DOCB	BA	16.10.91
2145	529	OO-SYG	SAB	31.10.91
2146	522	N916UA	UAL	23.10.91
2147	436	G-DOCC	BA	25.10.91
2148	405	LN-BRQ	Braa	24.10.91
2149	522	N917UA	UAL	29.10.91
2150	5Y0	B-2546	GPA	29.10.91
2151	530	D-ABJI	Luft	31.10.91
2152	522	N918UA	UAL	31.10.91
2153	33A	F-OGRT	Ansett	31.10.91
2153	33A	N33AW	Ansett	12.11.91
2154	522	N919UA	UAL	1.11.91
2155	5Y0	B-2547	GPA	1.11.91
2156	436	G-DOCD	BA	6.11.91
2157	5B6	CN-RMV	RAMar	12.11.91
2158	330	D-ABEI	Luft	7.11.91
2159	53A	LZ-BOC	Ansett	6.12.91
2160	484	SX-BKE	Olymp	14.11.91
2161	406	PH-BTA	KLM	16.11.91
2162	476	VH-TJL	AusA	12.11.91
2163	529	OO-SYH	SAB	27.11.91
2164	330	D-ABEK	Luft	21.11.91
2165	529	OO-SYI	SAB	27.11.91
2166	5B6	CN-RMW	RAMar	21.11.91
2167	436	G-DOCE	BA	20.11.91
2168	3Y0	B-2528	GPA	21.11.91
2169	566	SU-GBJ	Egyp	25.11.91
2170	528	F-GJNC	AirF	26.11.91
2171	476	VH-TJM	AusA	26.11.91
2172	33A	N34AW	Ansett	4.12.91
2173	5Q8	SE-DNH	ILFC	2.12.91
2174	484	SX-BKF	Olymp	12.12.91
2175	330	D-ABEL	Luft	5.12.91
2176	4Y0	G-OBMM	GPA	6.12.91
2178	436	G-DOCF	BA	10.12.91
2179	522	N920UA	UAL	6.12.91
2180	528	F-GJND	AirF	12.12.91
2181	522	N921UA	UAL	20.12.91
2182	330	D-ABEM	Luft	12.12.91
2183	436	G-DOCG	BA	19.12.91
2184	406	PH-BTB	KLM	15.1.92
2185	436	G-DOCH	BA	19.12.91
2186	59D	SE-DNI	Lflyg	19.12.91
2187	36E	EC-705	VIVA	14.1.92
2188	436	G-DOCI	BA	8.1.92
2189	522	N922UA	UAL	6.1.92
2190	522	N923UA	UAL	6.1.92
2191	528	F-GJNE	AirF	9.1.92
2192	3Q8	CS-TII	ILFC	8.1.92
2193	3Q8	G-OBMP	ILFC	10.1.92
2194	36E	EC-706	VIVA	15.1.92
2195	4Q8	VR-CAA	ILFC	13.1.92
2196	330	D-ABEN	Luft	16.1.92
2197	436	G-DOCJ	BA	16.1.92
2198	33A	N3213T	Ansett	23.1.92
2199	4Y0	N601TR	GPA	21.1.92
2200	406	PH-BTC	KLM	6.2.92
2201	4Y0	EC-936	GPA	21.1.92
2202	5H4	N522SW	SWA	21.1.92
2203	4Y0	TC-JDG	GPA	3.2.92
2204	5H4	N523SW	SWA	23.1.92
2205	3Y0	XA-RJR	GPA	12.2.92
2206	33A	EC-970	Ansett	19.3.92
2207	330	D-ABEO	Luft	7.2.92
2208	528	F-GJNF	AirF	31.1.92
2209	5B6	CN-RMY	RAMar	13.3.92
2210	4Q8	G-BSNV	ILFC	5.2.92
2211	5Y0	B-2548	GPA	3.2.92
2212	522	N924UA	UAL	7.2.92
2213	505	LN-BRR	Braa	7.2.92
2214	522	N925UA	UAL	6.2.92
2215	4C9	LX-LGF	Luxair	21.2.92
2216	330	D-ABEP	Luft	13.3.92
2217	429	OO-SBM	Sobel	14.2.92
2218	5Y0	B-2549	GPA	14.2.92
2219	4B6	CN-RMX	RAMar	13.3.92
2220	5Y0	XA-RJS	GPA	18.2.92
2221	4Q8	TC-AFM	ILFC	19.2.92
2222	436	G-DOCK	BA	25.2.92
2223	4S3	9M-MLJ	AOF	18.2.92
2224	5H4	N524SW	SWA	27.2.92
2225	505	LN-BRS	Braa	21.2.92
2226	382	CS-TIK	ILFC	25.2.92
2227	4Y0	TC-JDH	GPA	2.3.92
2228	436	G-DOCL	BA	2.3.92
2229	505	LN-BRT	Braa	27.2.92
2230	522	N926UA	UAL	2.3.92
2231	528	F-GJNG	AirF	6.3.92
2232	548	EI-CDF	AerL	27.3.92
2233	4S3	9M-MLG	AOF	5.3.92
2234	3L9	OY-MAK	MskA	6.3.92
2234	3L9	OY-MAL	MskA	30.3.92
2235	3B3	N854WT	UTA	9.3.92
2236	5Y0	XA-RKP	GPA	11.3.92
2237	4Q8	G-BSNW	ILFC	12.3.92
2238	5Y0	B-2550	GPA	12.3.92
2239	4Q8	G-OBMO	ILFC	13.3.92
2240	5Y0	XA-RKQ	GPA	13.3.92
2241	382	CS-TIL	ILFC	13.3.92
2242	330	D-ABER	Luft	20.3.92

Line No	Type No	First Owner Reg	First Owner	Delivery
2243	53C	F-GINL	EurI	18.3.92
2244	436	G-DOCM	BA	19.3.92
2245	505	LN-BRU	Braa	20.3.92
2246	522	N927UA	UAL	23.3.92
2247	330	D-ABES	Luft	25.3.92
2248	3Y0	XA-SAB	GPA	26.3.92
2249	4C9	LX-LGG	Luxair	27.3.92
2251	528	F-GJNH	AirF	30.3.92
2252	3Z0	B-2530	ChSWA	16.4.92
2253	5H3	TS-IOG	TunisA	10.4.92
2254	3J6	B-2580	AirCh	22.4.92
2255	4S3	G-OBMK	ILFC	6.4.92
2256	4Y0	EC-991	GPA	8.4.92
2257	522	N928UA	UAL	8.4.92
2258	4Y0	N600SK	GPA	9.4.92
2259	522	N929UA	UAL	10.4.92
2260	5Y0	XA-SAS	GPA	10.4.92
2261	548	EI-CDG	AerL	27.4.92
2262	5Y0	XA-SAC	GPA	14.4.92
2263	3J6	B-2581	AirCh	16.4.92
2264	4Q8	H4-SOL	ILFC	17.4.92
2265	476	VH-TJN	AusA	22.4.92
2266	4Q8	N754AS	ILFC	17.4.92
2267	3B3	N4361V	UTA	22.4.92
2268	3Q8	CS-TIJ	ILFC	23.4.92
2269	448	EI-BXK	AerL	23.4.92
2270	4Y0	G-UKLG	AUKL	23.4.92
2271	548	EI-CDH	AerL	14.4.92
2272	4H6	9M-MMA	MAS	30.4.92
2273	341	PP-VPA	GPA	20.5.92
2274	522	N930UA	UAL	28.4.92
2275	341	B-2594	ChYA	17.8.92
2276	566	SU-GBK	Egyp	1.5.92
2277	3L9	OY-MAM	MskA	7.5.92
2278	4Q8	N755AS	ILFC	5.5.92
2279	59D	SE-DNK	Lflyg	11.5.92
2280	4Q8	TC-JDI	ILFC	8.5.92
2282	566	SU-GBL	Egyp	8.5.92
2283	5H4	N525SW	SWA	26.5.92
2284	4Y0	TC-JDY	GPA	18.6.92
2285	5H4	N526SW	SWA	22.5.92
2286	5Y0	TC-JDU	GPA	16.6.92
2287	5H4	N527SW	SWA	28.5.92
2289	522	N931UA	UAL	21.5.92
2290	4Q8	CC-CYJ	ILFC	21.5.92
2291	522	N932UA	UAL	26.5.92
2292	5H4	N528SW	SWA	29.5.92
2293	522	N933UA	UAL	27.5.92
2294	3H4	N357SW	SWA	27.5.92
2295	3H4	N358SW	SWA	1.6.92
2296	529	OO-SYJ	SAB	1.6.92
2297	3H4	N359SW	SWA	3.6.92
2298	529	OO-SYK	SAB	5.6.92
2299	4Q8	N756AS	ILFC	5.6.92
2300	529	OK-XGA	CSA	15.6.92
2301	4Y0	TC-JDZ	GPA	19.6.92
2302	3K9	N41069	BFlug	9.6.92
2303	341	B-2908	ChXA	15.4.93
2304	5Y0	DQ-FJB	GPA	11.6.92
2305	341	EK-A001	NSA	12.11.92
2306	3Y0	B-2539	GPA	15.6.92
2307	3H4	N360SW	SWA	15.6.92
2308	4H6	9M-MMB	MAS	12.6.92
2309	3H4	N361SW	SWA	18.6.92
2310	33A	B-4018	Ansett	23.6.92
2311	430	D-ABKA	Luft	2.7.92
2312	522	N934UA	UAL	26.6.92
2313	33A	B-4019	Ansett	24.6.92
2314	48E	HL7227	Asiana	2.7.92
2315	522	N935UA	UAL	26.6.92
2316	430	D-ABKB	Luft	11.7.92
2317	529	OK-XGB	CSA	6.7.92
2318	4D7	HS-TDD	Thai	10.7.92
2319	529	OK-XGc	CSA	10.7.92
2320	4Q8	N760AS	ILFC	10.7.92
2321	341	PP-VPB	BFlug	7.7.92
2322	3H4	N362SW	SWA	9.7.92
2323	430	D-ABKC	Luft	16.7.92
2324	476	VH-TJO	AusA	13.7.92
2325	522	N936UA	UAL	15.7.92
2326	341	PP-VPC	BFlug	24.7.92
2327	5H6	9M-MFA	MAS	13.7.92
2328	430	D-ABKD	Luft	23.7.92
2329	522	N937UA	UAL	20.7.92
2330	4D7	HS-TDE	Thai	22.7.92
2331	3K9	N4113D	BFlug	24.7.92
2332	4H6	9M-MMC	MAS	20.7.92
2333	33A	N401AW	Ansett	11.12.92
2334	4Q8	N762AS	ILFC	13.7.92
2335	48E	HL7228	Asiana	24.7.92
2336	522	N938UA	UAL	30.7.92
2337	529	OK-XGD	CSA	31.7.92
2338	4D7	HS-TDF	Thai	5.6.92
2339	529	OK-XGE	CSA	7.8.92
2340	4H6	9M-MMD	MAS	4.8.92
2341	33A	AP-BEH	Ansett	8.9.92
2342	33A	N402AW	Ansett	15.12.92
2343	522	N939UA	UAL	7.8.92
2344	430	D-ABKF	Luft	13.8.92
2345	522	N940UA	UAL	10.9.92
2346	4Q8	N763AS	ILFC	20.8.92
2347	3L9	OY-MAN	MskA	25.9.92
2348	4Q8	N764AS	ILFC	21.9.92
2349	3Y0	B-2524	GPA	3.9.92
2350	4Q8	N765AS	ILFC	28.10.92
2351	505	LN-BRV	Braa	1.9.92
2352	4Y0	UR-GAA	GPA	2.11.92
2353	505	LN-BRW	Braa	8.9.92
2354	490	N767AS	AlaskA	9.9.92
2355	3Q8	5W-ILF	ILFC	8.9.92
2356	490	N768AS	AlaskA	10.9.92
2357	3Z0	B-2586	ChSWA	11.9.92
2358	5H6	9M-MFB	MAS	14.9.92
2359	430	D-ABKK	Luft	17.9.92
2360	33A	N403AW	Ansett	10.12.92
2361	4Y0	UR-GAB	GPA	13.11.92
2362	4H6	9M-MME	MAS	22.9.92
2363	476	VH-TJP	AusA	21.9.92
2364	522	N941UA	UAL	6.10.92
2365	522	N942UA	UAL	28.10.92
2366	522	N943UA	UAL	2.11.92
2367	430	D-ABKL	Luft	1.10.92
2368	522	N944UA	UAL	3.11.92
2369	3Y0	B-2595	GPA	7.10.92
2370	3Z0	B-2590	ChSWA	29.9.92
2371	476	VH-TJQ	AusA	29.9.92
2372	4H6	9M-MMF	MAS	5.10.92
2373	33A	N404AW	Ansett	11.12.92
2374	5Y0	PT-SLN	GPA	23.10.9
2375	4Y0	TC-JER	GPA	9.4.9
2376	4Y0	TC-JES	GPA	21.4.9
2377	3W0	B-2589	ChYA	3.11.9
2378	4H6	9M-MMG	MAS	16.10.9
2379	436	G-DOCN	BA	21.10.9
2380	4Q8	N401KW	ILFC	20.10.9
2381	436	G-DOCO	BA	26.10.9
2382	497	N401AL	Aloha	2.11.9
2383	3Q8	N373TA	ILFC	22.10.9
2384	3J6	B-2585	AirCh	21.12.9
2385	3J6	B-2584	AirCh	21.12.9
2386	436	G-DOCP	BA	2.11.9
2387	436	G-DOCR	BA	6.11.9
2388	522	N945UA	UAL	1.12.9
2390	436	G-DOCS	BA	1.12.9
2391	4H6	9M-MMH	MAS	12.11.9
2393	497	N402AL	Aloha	13.11.9
2394	4K5	D-AHLM	HL	19.3.9
2395	4H6	9M-MMI	MAS	23.11.9
2396	3J6	B-2587	AirCh	29.1.9
2398	476	VH-TJR	AusA	25.11.9
2399	4H6	9M-MMJ	MAS	4.12.9
2400	3W0	B-2540	YunnPA	11.1.9
2402	522	N946UA	UAL	16.12.9
2403	4H6	9M-MMK	MAS	14.12.9
2404	522	N947UA	UAL	11.12.9
2405	3Y9	N999CZ	C Itoh	26.1.9
2407	4H6	9M-MML	MAS	22.12.9
2408	522	N948UA	UAL	21.12.9
2409	436	G-DOCT	BA	22.12.9
2410	4H6	9M-MMM	MAS	8.1.9
2411	528	F-GJNI	AirF	7.1.9
2412	59D	SE-DNL	SAS	8.1.9
2413	5C9	LX-LGO	Luxair	8.1.9
2414	33A	N405AW	Ansett	22.3.9
2415	3H6	9M-MZA	MAS	15.1.9
2416	4Q8	N402KW	ILFC	14.1.9
2417	436	G-DOCU	BA	18.1.9
2389	55D	SP-LKA	LOT	22.12.9
2392	55D	SP-LKB	LOT	22.12.9
2397	55D	SP-LKC	LOT	22.12.9
2401	55D	SP-LKD	LOT	22.12.9
2406	306	PH-BTD	KLM	18.12.9
2418	3Q8	N571LF	ILFC	8.2.9
2419	4H6	9M-MMN	MAS	26.1.9
2420	436	G-DOCV	BA	25.1.9
2421	522	N949UA	UAL	1.2.93
2422	436	G-DOCW	BA	2.2.93
2423	522	N950UA	UAL	1.2.93
2424	3Q8	N374TA	ILFC	1.2.93
2425	4Y0	TC-JET	GPA	9.4.93
2426	4H6	9M-MMO	MAS	9.2.93
2427	548	EI-CDS	ILFC	9.2.93
2428	528	F-GJNJ	AirF	11.2.93
2429	3H4	N363SW	SWA	10.2.93
2430	3H4	N364SW	SWA	12.2.93
2431	4Y0	TC-JEU	GPA	16.4.93
2432	4Z9	OE-LNI	Lauda	23.2.93
2433	3H4	N365SW	SWA	17.2.93
2435	4H6	9M-MMP	MAS	1.3.93
2436	3Z0	3B-2533	ChSWA	1.3.93
2437	31B	B-2596	ChSA	1.3.93
2438	306	PH-BTE	KLM	6.3.93

Line No	Type No	First Owner Reg	First Owner	Delivery
439	332	N301DE	Delta	20.3.93
440	522	N951UA	UAL	8.3.93
441	4H6	9M-MMQ	MAS	30.3.93
442	4Y0	D-ABAF	GPA	10.3.93
443	528	F-GJNK	AirF	12.3.93
444	5C9	LX-LGP	Luxair	16.3.93
445	4H6	9M-MMR	MAS	19.3.93
446	3Y5	9H-ABR	AirM	26.3.93
447	4Q8	G-BUHJ	ILFC	11.3.93
448	55D	SP-LKE	LOT	23.3.93
449	505	LN-BRY	Braa	23.3.93
450	4H6	9M-MMS	MAS	1.4.93
451	436	G-DOCX	BA	29.3.93
452	4Q8	N769AS	ILFC	31.3.93
453	4B6	CN-RNA	RAMar	8.4.93
454	476	VH-TJS	AusA	4.5.93
455	332	N302DE	Delta	7.4.93
456	3Y0	B-2909	GPA	16.4.93;
457	42J	TC-JEA	ArabL	16.4.93
458	45D	SP-LLA	LOT	13.4.93
459	3Y0	B-2910	GPA	16.4.93;
460	3Y0	B-2911	GPA	20.4.93;
461	4Q8	TC-JED	ILFC	21.4.93
462	4H6	9M-MMT	MAS	27.4.93
463	548	EI-CDT	ILFC	23.4.94
464	528	F-GJNM	AirF	27.4.93
465	46J	D-ABAE	ABer	18.4.93
466	3Q8	CS-TIM	ILFC	30.4.93
467	3Y5	9H-ABS	AirM	30.4.93
468	4Y0	TC-JEV	GPA	6.5.93
469	3H4	N366SW	SWA	5.5.93
470	3H4	N367SW	SWA	7.5.93
471	484	SX-BKG	Olymp	3.6.93
472	5B6	CN-RNB	RAMar	14.5.93
473	3H4	N368SW	SWA	13.5.93
474	5H3	TS-IOH	TunisA	21.5.93
475	4Y0	TC-JEY	GPA	18.5.93
476	4Q8	N771AS	ILFC	21.5.93
477	3H4	N369SW	SWA	21.5.93
478	3Y5	9H-ABT	AirM	25.5.93

Line No	Type No	First Owner Reg	First Owner	Delivery
2481	4D7	HS-TDG	Thai	27.5.93
2482	4Q8	TC-JEE	ILFC	3.6.93
2483	4L7	C2-RN10	AirN	9.6.93
2484	5H6	9M-MFC	MAS	11.6.93
2485	522	N952UA	UAL	14.6.93
2486	4Q8	G-BUHK	ILFC	14.6.93
2487	4Y0	TC-JEZ	GPA	16.6.93
2488	332	N303DE	Delta	16.6.93
2489	3J6	B-2588	AirCh	25.6.93
2490	522	N953UA	UAL	23.6.93
2491	4H6	9M-MMV	MAS	24.6.93
2492	45D	SP-LLB	LOT	25.6.93
2493	3J6	B-2598	AirCh	25.6.93
2494	522	N954UA	UAL	2.7.93
2495	3Z0	B-2597	ChSWA	30.6.93
2496	4H6	9M-MMW	MAS	26.7.93
2497	3H4	N370SW	SWA	2.7.93
2498	522	N955UA	UAL	12.7.93
2499	31B	B-2582	ChSA	2.8.93
2500	3H4	N371SW	SWA	13.7.93
2501	4H6	9M-MMX	MAS	20.7.93
2502	45D	SP-LLC	LOT	20.7.93
2503	5H6	9M-MFD	MAS	28.7.93
2504	3H4	N372SW	SWA	21.7.93
2505	4Q8	N772AS	ILFC	27.7.93
2506	332	N304DE	Delta	2.8.93
2507	4H6	9M-MMY	MAS	12.8.93
2508	522	N956UA	UAL	2.8.93
2509	3H4	N373SW	SWA	2.8.93
2510	332	N305DE	Delta	6.8.93
2511	5H6	9M-MFE	MAS	13.8.93
2512	522	N957UA	UAL	9.8.93
2513	4Q8	TC-JEF	ILFC	9.8.93
2514	436	G-BVBY	BA	2.9.93
2515	3H4	N374SW	SWA	12.8.93
2516	505	LN-BRZ	Braa	1.9.93
2517	4L7	C2-RN11	AirN	27.8.93
2518	4Q8	N773AS	ILFC	2.9.93
2519	3Q8	B-2903	ILFC	3.9.93
2520	3H4	N375SW	SWA	7.9.93

Line No	Type No	First Owner Reg	First Owner	Delivery
2521	4H6	9M-MMZ	MAS	30.9.93
2522	436	G-BVBZ	BA	1.10.93
2523	3Q8	B-2920	ChSA	14.9.93
2524	38J	YR-BGA	Tarom	18.10.93
2525	4H6	9M-MQA	MAS	29.10.93
2526	4Q8	N774AS	ILFC	1.10.93
2527	5H6	9M-MFF	MAS	29.9.93
2528	3Q8	B-2921	ChSA	24.9.93
2529	38J	R-BGB	Tarom	18.10.93
2530	4H6	9M-MQB	MAS	29.10.93
2531	4U3	PK-GWK	Garuda	15.10.93
2532	436	G-BVHA	BA	1.11.93
2533	4H6	9M-MQC	MAS	29.10.93
2534	5Y0	PT-SLP	GPA	14.10.93
2535	4U3	PK-GWL	Garuda	23.12.93
2536	4H6	9M-MQD	MAS	9.11.93
2537	4U3	PK-GWM	Garuda	25.10.93
2538	5Y0	B-2912	GPA	21.3.94
2539	476	VH-TJT	Qantas	18.10.93
2540	4U3	PK-GWN	Garuda	1.11.93
2541	3Q8	N351LF	ILFC	22.10.93
2542	4H6	9M-MQE	MAS	2.12.93
2543	48E	HL7231	Asiana	10.1.94
2544	5Y0	B-2915	GPA	21.3.94
2545	436	G-BVHB	BA	2.12.93
2546	4U3	PK-GWO	Garuda	9.11.93
2547	37K	B-2935	ZhoA	1.2.94
2548	4U3	PK-GWP	Garuda	23.12.93
2549	4U3	PK-GWQ	Garuda	23.12.93
2550	3Q8	N261LF	ILFC	3.12.93
2551	4Q8	N775AS	ILFC	3.12.93
2552	5Y0	PT-SLS	GPA	15.12.93
2553	5Y0	PT-SLT	GPA	14.1.94
2554	31B	B-2583	ChSA	3.12.93
2555	31B	B-2922	ChSA	6.12.93
2556	31L	B-2930	ChXinA	9.12.93

BELOW: Alaska 737-400 N782AS about to land at Orange County with a sister ship in the background.

119

Line No	Type No	First Owner Reg	First Owner	Delivery
2557	3Q8	B-2937	ILFC	10.12.93
2558	3Z0	B-2599	ChSWA	14.12.93
2559	39K	B-2934	ChXinA	21.12.93
2560	4H6	9M-MQF	MAS	10.1.94
2561	4Q8	N776AS	ILFC	10.1.94
2562	4Q8	TC-JEG	ILFC	7.1.94
2563	4Q8	TC-JEH	ILFC	11.1.94
2564	4Q8	TC-JEI	ILFC	1.3.94
2565	31B	B-2923	ChSA	11.1.94
2566	524	N14601	CAL	11.2.94
2567	31L	B-2931	ChXA	31.1.94
2568	4H6	9M-MQG	MAS	1.2.94
2569	476	VH-TJU	Qantas	19.1.94
2570	3H4	N376SW	SWA	21.1.94
2571	524	N69602	CAL	7.2.94
2572	528	F-GJNN	AirF	4.2.94
2573	524	N69603	CAL	11.2.94
2574	528	F-GJNO	AirF	10.2.94
2575	31B	B-2924	ChSA	22.2.94
2576	524	N14604	CAL	15.2.94
2577	31B	B-2925	ChSA	25.2.94
2578	505	LN-BUA	ILFC	21.2.94
2579	3H4	N378SW	SWA	18.2.94
2580	3H4	N379SW	SWA	22.2.94
2581	3Q8	B-2938	ILFC	23.2.94
2582	524	N14605	CAL	2.3.94
2583	5H3	TS-IOI	TunisA	1.3.94
2584	4B6	CN-RNC	RAMar	3.5.94
2585	46J	D-ABAG	FlugHS	7.3.94
2586	4Q8	N777AS	ILFC	14.3.94
2587	3L9	OY-MAO	MskA	11.3.94
2588	4B6	CN-RND	RAMar	3.5.94
2589	45D	SP-LLD	LOT	18.3.94
2590	524	N58606	CAL	21.3.94
2591	406	PH-BTF	KLM	25.3.94
2592	59D	SE-DNM	SAS	24.3.94
2593	31B	B-2926	ChSA	31.3.94
2594	3L9	OY-MAP	MskA	25.3.94
2595	31B	B-2927	ChSA	31.3.94
2596	524	N16607	CAL	6.4.94
2597	524	N36608	CAL	5.4.94
2598	4Q8	TC-JEJ	ILFC	7.4.94
2599	33A	B-2947	Ansett	14.4.94
2600	33A	VH-CZU	Ansett	19.4.94
2601	406	PH-BTG	KLM	20.4.94
2602	4Q8	TC-JEK	ILFC	19.4.94
2603	55D	SP-LKF	LOT	5.5.94
2604	4Q8	TC-JEL	ILFC	2.5.94
2605	4Q8	N779AS	ILFC	28.4.94
2606	33A	CS-TKF	Ansett	16.5.94
2607	524	N14609	CAL	5.5.94
2608	33A	CS-TKG	Ansett	17.5.94
2609	37K	B-2936	ZhoA	22.11.94
2610	3H4	N380SW	SWA	12.5.94
2611	3H4	N382SW	SWA	13.5.94
2612	3H4	N383SW	SWA	16.5.94
2613	3H4	N384SW	SWA	19.5.94
2614	58E	HL7232	Asiana	25.5.94
2615	3H6	9M-MZB	MAS	27.5.94
2616	524	N27610	CAL	31.5.94
2617	3H4	N385SW	SWA	31.5.94
2618	4Q3	JA8523	JTA	13.6.94
2619	31B	B-2929	ChSA	9.6.94
2620	4Q8	TC-JEM	ILFC	9.6.94
2621	524	N18611	CAL	14.6.94
2622	31B	B-2941	ChSA	16.6.94
2623	3Q8	EC-547	ILFC	17.6.94
2624	4H6	9M-MQH	MAS	23.6.94
2625	31L	B-2939	ChXinA	11.7.94
2626	3H4	N386SW	SWA	27.6.94
2627	3H4	N387SW	SWA	29.6.94
2628	3H4	N388SW	SWA	1.7.94
2629	3H4	N389SW	SWA	6.7.94
2630	524	N11612	CAL	19.7.94
2631	3J6	B-2948	AirCh	15.7.94
2632	4H6	9M-MQI	MAS	18.7.94
2633	524	N14613	CAL	25.7.94
2634	524	N17614	CAL	30.8.94
2635	3Q8	HA-LEJ	ILFC	22.7.94
2636	31L	B-2940	ChXinA	27.7.94
2637	5H6	49M-MFG	MAS	1.8.94
2638	4Q8	N780AS	ILFC	2.8.94
2639	37K	B-2945	ChXha	16.8.94
2640	524	N37615	CAL	9.8.94
2641	524	N52616	CAL	10.8.94
2642	3H4	N390SW	SWA	8.94
2643	3H4	N391SW	SWA	2.9.94
2644	3H4	N392SW	SWA	8.9.94
2645	3H4	N394SW	SWA	12.9.94
2646	5H6	9M-MFH	MAS	9.9.94
2647	3Z0	B-2950	ChSWA	12.9.94
2648	524	N16617	CAL	16.9.94
2649	505	LN-BUC	ILFC	15.9.94
2650	3J6	B-2949	AirCh	5.10.94
2651	3Q8	5R-MFH	ILFC	12.9.94
2652	524	N16618	CAL	26.9.94
2653	4Q8	TC-AFA	ILFC	3.10.94
2654	5H6	9M-MFI	MAS	3.10.94
2655	37K	B-2946	ZhoA	22.11.94
2656	4Q8	N782AS	ILFC	14.10.94
2657	4H6	9M-MQJ	MAS	1.11.94
2658	3Z0	B-2951	ChSWA	1.11.94
2659	524	N17619	CAL	28.10.94
2660	524	N17620	CAL	21.2.95
2661	524	N19621	CAL	5.12.94
2662	38J	YR-BGC	Tarom	7.11.94
2663	38J	YR-BGD	Tarom	7.11.94
2664	3Q8	N721LF	ILFC	1.11.94
2665	4Q8	HL7235	ILFC	31.10.94
2666	4Q8	N783AS	ILFC	1.12.94
2667	3H4	N395SW	SWA	4.11.94
2668	3H4	N396SW	SWA	8.11.94
2669	524	N18622	CAL	8.12.94
2670	4K5	D-AHLT	HL	14.11.94
2671	38J	YR-BGE	Tarom	18.11.94
2672	524	N19623	CAL	26.1.95
2673	4H6	9M-MQK	MAS	7.12.94
2674	3Q8	N73380	ILFC	5.12.94
2675	524	N13624	CAL	7.2.95
2676	4H6	9M-MQL	MAS	10.1.95
2677	4K5	D-AHLU	HL	7.12.94
2678	31B	B-2952	ChSA	9.12.94
2679	33A	F-ODZY	Ansett	13.12.94
2680	3Q8	N14381	ILFC	6.1.95
2681	3Q8	N19382	ILFC	9.1.95
2682	330	D-ABET	Luft	12.1.95
2683	524	N46625	CAL	27.1.9
2685	4H6	9M-MQM	Malay	1.2.9
2686	524	N32626	CAL	13.4.9
2687	33A	B-2955	Ansett	15.2.9
2688	3L9	OY-MAR	MskA	6.2.9
2689	4Q8	TC-JEN	ILFC	31.1.9
2690	33A	B-2956	Ansett	22.2.9
2691	330	D-ABEU	Luft	2.2.9
2692	3L9	OY-MAS	MskA	21.2.9
2693	3Q8	N14383	ILFC	9.2.9
2694	4Q3	JA8524	JTA	1.2.9
2694	46J	D-ABAH	FlugHS	8.2.9
2695	3H4	N397SW	SWA	15.1.9
2696	3H4	N398SW	SWA	17.2.9
2697	3H4	N399WN	SWA	23.2.9
2698	4Z6	HS-RTA	RThAF	28.2.9
2699	3H4	N600WN	SWA	28.2.9
2700	524	N17627	CAL	14.4.9
2701	5H3	TS-IOJ	TunisA	9.3.9
2702	3H4	N601WN	SWA	10.3.9
2703	33A	VH-CZT	Ansett	3.4.9
2704	3Q8	N14384	ILFC	20.3.9
2705	330	D-ABEW	Luft	23.3.9
2706	36E	EC-796	ILFC	27.3.9
2707	3Q8	N73385	ILFC	28.3.9
2708	54K	JA8404	Nippon	12.4.9
2709	33A	OO-LTU	Ansett	4.4.9
2710	3J6	B-2953	AirCh	27.4.9
2711	4K5	D-AHLG	ILFC	5.4.9
2712	524	N14628	CAL	19.4.9
2713	3H4	N602SW	SWA	19.4.9
2714	3H4	N603SW	SWA	21.4.9
2715	3H4	N604SW	SWA	25.4.9
2716	3H4	N605SW	SWA	27.4.9
2717	4Q8	TC-JEO	ILFC	2.5.9
2718	446	JA8991	JAL	31.5.9
2719	36E	EC-797	ILFC	10.5.9
2720	528	LX-LGR	ILC	18.8.95
2721	3K2	PH-TSZ	ILFC	17.5.9
2722	3K2	PH-TSY	ILFC	30.5.9
2723	54K	JA8419	Nippon	28.7.9
2724	58E	HL7233	Asiana	19.5.9
2725	524	N14629	CAL	26.5.9
2726	524	N59630	CAL	30.5.9
2727	3W0	B-2958	ChYA	6.6.9
2728	524	N62631	CAL	12.6.9
2729	446	JA8992	JAL	28.6.9
2730	4Q8	TC-JEP	ILFC	21.6.9
2730	528	LX-LGS	ILC	15.9.9
2731	3Q8	PH-TSX	ILFC	28.6.9
2733	4B6	CN-RNF	RAMar	15.7.95
2734	5B6	CN-RNG	RAMar	15.7.95
2735	5Q8	ES-ABC	ILFC	6.95
2736	524	N16632	CAL	11.7.95
2737	58E	HL7250	Asiana	13.7.95
2738	3Z0	B-2957	ChSWA	18.7.95
2739	528	PRP-001	PAF	1.9.95
2740	3H4	N606SW	SWA	24.7.95
2741	3H4	N607SW	SWA	26.7.95
2742	3H4	N608SW	SWA	31.7.95
2743	524	N24633	CAL	4.8.95
2744	3H4	N609SW	SWA	4.8.95
2745	3H4	N610WN	SWA	24.8.95

Line No	Type No	First Owner Reg	First Owner	Delivery
746	34N	B-4020	NCA	1.9.95
747	34N	B-4021	NCA	1.9.95
748	524	N19634	ILFC	31.8.95
749	33A	9M-LKY	Ansett	11.9.95
750	3H4	N611SW	SWA	12.9.95
750	33A	9V-TRE	Ansett	3.10.95
751	54K	JA8500	Nippon	19.9.95
752	4Q3	JA8525	JAL	18.9.95
753	3H4	N612SW	SWA	23.9.95
754	3H4	N613SW	SWA	26.9.95
755	3H4	N614SW	SWA	29.9.95
757	3H4	N615SW	SWA	6.10.95
758	3H4	N616SW	SWA	10.10.95
759	3H4	N617SW	SWA	30.10.95
761	3H4	N618WN	SWA	1.11.95
762	3H4	N619SW	SWA	9.11.95
762	3L9	OY-MAT	MskA	14.10.95
763	3L9	OY-MAU	MskA	18.11.95;
764	3Q8	N17386	ILFC	18.12.95
765	33A	B-2966	Ansett	25.1.96
766	3H4	N620SW	SWA	12.1.96
767	3H4	N621SW	SWA	19.1.96;
768	3J6	B-2954	AirCh	29.1.96
769	36E	EC-798	ILFC	12.2.96
770	5Q8	ES-ABD	ILFC	9.2.96
771	524	N33635	ILFC	14.2.96
772	3Q8	B-2963	ILFC	19.2.96
773	476	VH-TJX	Qantas	23.2.96
774	35H	B-2961	ShA	6.3.96
775	31B	B-2959	ChSA	7.3.96
776	524	N33637	CAL	2.4.96
777	524	N19636	ILFC	3.4.96
778	35H	B-2962	ShA	26.3.96
779	3H4	N622SW	SWA	20.3.96
780	3H4	N623SW	SWA	25.3.96
781	3H4	N624SW	SWA	27.2.96
782	4Q8	B-2965	ILFC	2.4.96
783	54K	JA8504	Nippon	17.5.96
784	5L9	OY-APA	MskA	8.4.96
785	476	VH-TJY	Qantas	12.4.96
2786	3Q8	N661LF	ILFC	17.4.96
2787	3H4	N625SW	SWA	23. 4.96
2788	5L9	OY-APB	MskA	244.96
2789	3H4	N626SW	SWA	1.5.96
2790	3H4	N627SW	SWA	6.5.96
2791	48E	HL7508	Asiana	8.5.96
2792	36E	EC-799	ILFC	14.5.96
2793	4Q8	B-2967	ILFC	17.5.96
2794	46J	D-ABAI	ABer	21.5.96
2795	3H4	N628SW	SWA	30.5.96
2796	3H4	N629SW	SWA	6.6.96
2797	3H4	N630WN	SWA	5.6.96
2798	3H4	N631SW	SWA	10.6.96
2799	3H4	N632SW	SWA	13.6.96
2800	505	LN-BUE	ILFC	17.6.96
2801	46J	D-ABAK	ABer	24.6.96
2802	46J	D-ABAL	ABer	30.6.96
2803	505	LN-BUA	Braa	29.7.96
2804	45D	SP-LLE	LOT	12.7.96
2805	505	B-2973	ILFC	18.7.96
2806	48E	HL7509	ILFC	23.7.96
2807	3H4	N633SW	SWA	29.7.96
2808	3H4	N634SW	SWA	5.8.96
2809	36M	OO-VEA	BAHC	16.8.96
2810	36M	OO-VEB	DML	22.8.96
2811	4Q8	B-2970	ILFC	21.8.96
2812	446	JA8993	JAL	27.8.96
2813	3H4	N635SW	SWA	3.9.96
2814	3H4	N636WN	SWA	9.9.96
2815	54K	JA8195	Nippon	13.9.96
2816	48E	HL7510	Asiana	20.9.96
2817	5L9	OY-MAF	MskA	23.9.96
2818	35H	B-2968	ShA	22.10.96
2819	3H4	N637SW	SWA	3.10.96
2820	3H4	N638SW	SWA	4.10.96
2821	3H4	N639SW	SWA	7.10.96
2822	505	B-2975	ChXA	16.10.96
2823	5L9	OY-APC	MskA	17.10.96
2824	54K	JA8196	Nippon	23.10.96
2825	5L9	OY-APD	MskA	24.10.96
2826	4Q8	N784AS	ILFC	19.11.96
2827	43Q	B-18671	GECAS	22.11.96
2828	5L9	OY-APG	MskA	12.11.96
2829	476	VH-TJZ	Qantas	8.11.96
2830	43Q	B-18672	GECAS	22.11.96
2831	33A	B-2972	Ansett	22.11.96
2832	43Q	B-18673	GECAS	22.11.96
2833	49R	N460PR	GECC	27.6.97
2834	5Q8	PT-SSB	ILFC	5.12.96
2835	36N	G-ECAS	GECAS	16.12.96
2836	3A1	CP-2313	VASP	20.12.96
2837	43Q	B-18675	BAHC	19.12.96
2838	43Q	B-18676	BAHC	19.12.96
2839	43Q	B-18677	BAHC	20.12.96
2840	3H4	N640SW	SWA	19.12.96
2841	3H4	N641SW	SWA	20.12.96
2842	3H4	N642WN	SWA	8.1.97
2843	3H4	N643SW	SWA	13.1.97
2844	46M	OO-VEC	Virgin	17.1.97
2845	49R	N461PR	ProA	9.6.97
2846	36N	9M-MAB	GECAS	27.1.97
2847	46M	OO-VED	Virgin	27.1.97
2848	48E	HL7511	ILFC	31.1.97
2849	55S	OK-CGH	CSA	12.3.97
2850	54K	JA8595	Nippon	19.2.97
2852	4H6	9M-MQN	Malay	3.3.97
2853	54K	JA8596	Nippon	24.2.97
2854	3Q8	HB-IIG	ILFC	14.2.97
2855	5B6	CN-RNH	RAMar	28.2.97
2856	5L9	OY-APH	MskA	24.2.97
2857	48E	HL7512	ILFC	25.2.97
2858	4Q8	N785AS	ILFC	28.2.97
2858	36N	9M-TRF	GECAS	14.2.97
2859	36Q	B-2982	BAS	14.3.97
2860	48E	HL7513	Asiana	17.3.97

BELOW: Hapag-Lloyd has five series -500s delivered during 1990 and '91 alongside 12 -400s, and 16 -800s on order. Taxying for departure is 737-5K5 D-AHLE.

Line No	Type No	First Owner Reg	First Owner	Delivery	Line No	Type No	First Owner Reg	First Owner	Delivery	Line No	Type No	First Owner Reg	First Owner	Deliver
2861	55S	OK-CGJ	CSA	12.3.97	2925	48E	N775SR	SunAC	28.8.97	2988	3U3	PK-GGK	Garuda	
2862	36N	G-SMDB	GECAS	15.3.97	2926	524	N11641	CAL	29.8.97	2989	36Q	N307FL	BAS	4.2.98
2863	3U8	5Y-KQA	Kenya	27.3.97	2927	524	N16642	CAL	17.9.97	2990	490	N793AS	AlaskA	
2864	33A	OK-FAN	Ansett	26.3.97	2928	31S	D-ADBL	DBA	5.9.97	2991	58E	N291SR	SunAC	5.6.9
2865	36Q	EC-GMY	BAHC	4.4.97	2929	58N	FAC 921	ChAF	18.9.97	2992	3U3	N360PR	Hell	18.11.9
2866	505	LN-BUG	ILFC	25.3.97	2930	306	PH-BTH	KLM	8.10.97	2993	524	N14654	CAL	17.2.9
2867	405	LN-BUF	Braa	15.4.97	2931	3H4	N655WN	SWA	10.9.97	2994	524	N14655	CAL	12.2.9
2868	5L9	OY-API	MskA	25.3.97	2932	3H4	N656WN	SWA	26.9.97	2995	36N	F-GRFB	GECAS	
2869	3H4	N644SW	SWA	31.3.97	2933	524	N20643	CAL	24.9.97	2996	36N	F-GRFC	GECAS	
2870	3H4	N645SW	SWA	2.4.97	2934	524	N17644	CAL	29.9.97	2997	42R	TC-APD	PHT	27.3.9
2871	3H4	N646SW	SWA	4.4.97	2935	524	N14645	CAL	30.9.97	2998	5L9	OY-APL	MskA	17.2.9
2872	54K	JA300K	Nippon	19.5.97	2936	36N	PT-TEP	GECAS	14.11.97	3000	490	N794AS	AlaskA	
2873	33A	OK-FUN	Ansett	17.4.97	2937	5U3	PK-GGC	Garuda	26.12.97	3001	34S	G-OGBC	GBAir	
2874	45D	SP-LLF	LOT	23.4.97	2938	5U3	PK-GGD	Garuda	27.12.97	3002	54K	JA302K	Nippon	9.3.9
2875	54K	JA301K	Nippon	20.5.97	2939	36Q	B-2989	BAS	16.10.97	3003	3U3	N1790B	GECC	
2876	36N	G-OJTW	GECAS	26.4.97	2940	36Q	PP-VPQ	BAHC	22.10.97	3004	55S	OK-DGL	CSA	18.3.9
2877	4H6	9M-MQO	Malay	29.4.97	2941	3W0	B-2983	ChYA	23.10.97	3005	31S	D-ADBS	DBA	10.3.9
2878	3Q8	N304FL	ILFC	1.5.97	2942	31S	D-ADBM	DBA	24.10.97	3006	490	N795AS	AlaskA	12.3.9
2879	46J	D-ABAM	ABer	28.4.97	2943	45R	VT-JAR	Jet	12.11.97	3007	33A	9H-ADH	Ansett	12.3.9
2880	36Q	D-ADBX	BAHC	8.5.97	2944	56N	PT-SSD	GECAS	11.11.97	3008	5L9	OY-APN	MskA	23.3.9
2881	33R	N963WP	WTC	14.5.97	2945	3W0	B-2985	ChYA	12.11.97	3009	74Q8	TC-APP	ILFC	31.3.9
2882	36N	PH-OZC	GECAS	12.5.97	2946	31S	D-ADBN	DBA	4.11.97	3010	36N	CS-TGQ	GECAS	30.3.9
2883	36Q	EC-GNU	BAHC	13.5.97	2947	5L9	OY-APK	MskA	31.10.97	3011	36Q	PP-VPR	BAS	24.3.9
2884	3U8	5Y-KQB	Kenya	20.5.97	2948	36N	OO-VEX	GECAS	18.11.97	3012	33S	OO-SLK	PemCC	30.3.9
2885	55S	OK-CGK	CSA	23.5.97	2949	3U3	PK-GGG	Garuda	31.12.97	3013	36Q	ZK-NGB	BAHC	31.3.98
2886	46N	G-SFBH	GECAS	30.5.97	2950	5U3	PK-GGE	Garuda		3014	55S	OK-DGM	CSA	7.4.9
2887	33R	N964WP	BAS	27.6.97	2951	3W0	B-2986	ChYA	2.12.97	3015	45R	VT-JAT	Jet	27.3.9
2888	36N	B-2977	GECAS	29.5.97	2952	5U3	PK-GGF	Garuda	27.12.97	3017	54K	JA303K	Nippon	13.4.9
2889	5Q8	PT-SSC	ILFC	30.5.97	2953	446	JA8996	JAL	14.11.97	3018	4M0	VP-BAH	Aflot	1.5.9
2890	36N	SP-LMC	GECAS	12.6.97	2954	48E	HL7518	ILFC	18.11.97	3019	524	N11656	CAL	17.4.9
2891	490	N788AS	AlaskA	9.6.97	2955	36N	PP-VPS	GECAS	21.11.97	3020	36Q	YR-BGX	BAS	25.4.9
2892	3H4	N647SW	SWA	9.6.97	2956	524	N16646	CAL	1.12.97	3021	33A	9H-ADI	Ansett	22.4.9
2893	3H4	N648SW	SWA	20.6.97	2957	306	PH-BTI	KLM	17.12.97	3022	36N	OO-VEH	GECAS	28.4.9
2894	3H4	N649SW	SWA	9.6.97	2958	524	N16647	CAL	24.11.97	3023	36Q	G-OFRA	BAS	5.5.9
2895	45D	SP-LLG	LOT	19.6.97	2959	33A	TJ-CBG	Ansett	26.11.97	3024	5Q8	PT-SSG	ILFC	14.4.9
2896	36N	SP-LMD	GECAS	24.6.97	2960	524	N16648	CAL	5.12.97	3025	4M0	VP-BAI	Aflot	12.5.9
2897	36N	B-2978	GECAS	23.6.97	2961	37Q	G-OAMS	Novel	10.12.97	3026	524	N23657	CAL	8.5.9
2898	4Q3	JA8526	JAL	26.6.97	2962	4D7	HS-TDH	Thai	9.12.97	3027	490	N796AS	AlaskA	12.5.9
2899	33R	N965WP	GATX	27.6.97	2963	45R	VT-JAS	Jet	16.12.97	3028	45S	OK-DGN	CSA	18.5.9
2900	33R	N966WP	SunAC	2.7.97	2964	36N	PP-VPT	GECAS	9.12.97	3029	3U3	PK-GGN	Garuda	
2901	3H4	N650SW	SWA	30.6.97	2965	5Q8	PT-SSE	ILFC	11.12.97	3030	54K	JA304K	Nippon	19.5.98
2902	490	N791AS	AlaskA	10.7.97	2966	3U3	PK-GGH	Garuda		3031	36N	G-XBHX	GECAS	21.6.9
2903	490	N792AS	AlaskA	14.7.97	2967	31S	D-ADBO	DBA	18.12.97	3032	3U3	PK-GGO	Garuda	
2905	48E	N773SR	SunAC	8.8.97	2968	4D7	HS-TDJ	Thai	16.12.97	3033	43Q	TC-IAA	BAS	1.6.9
2906	39M	F-ODZZ	AirA	31.7.97	2969	3U3	PK-GGI	Garuda		3034	3U8	5Y-KQC	Kenya	29.5.9
2907	446	JA8994	JAL	22.7.97	2970	36R	B-2988	Wuhan	23.12.97	3035	36Q	G-OHAJ	BAHC	2.6.9
2908	36N	B-2979	GECAS	25.7.97	2971	36N	PP-VPU	GECAS	18.12.97	3036	490	N797AS	AlaskA	9.6.9
2909	48E	HL7517	Asiana	25.7.97	2972	524	N16649	CAL	19.12.97	3037	3U3	PK-GGP	Garuda	
2910	46Q	EC-GPI	BAHC	28.7.97	2973	524	N16650	CAL	23.12.97	3038	490	N799AS	AlaskA	6.6.9
2911	446	JA8995	JAL	29.7.97	2974	3U3	PK-GGJ	Garuda		3039	490	N703AS	AlaskA	11.6.9
2912	524	N19638	CAL	31.7.97	2975	33R	ZK-NGA	GECAS	9.1.98	3040	43Q	TC-IAB	BAS	12.6.9
2913	524	N14639	CAL	31.7.97	2976	36N	F-GRFA	GECAS	18.1.98	3041	36N	G-XMAN	GECAS	18.6.9
2914	36Q	N305FA	BAS	11.8.97	2977	4D7	HS-TDK	Thai	6.1.98	3042	490	N705AS	AlaskA	16.6.98
2915	3H4	N651SW	SWA	6.8.97	2978	4D7	HS-TDL	Thai	15.1.98	3043	4Q3	JA8597	JTA	18.6.9
2916	3H4	N652SW	SWA	8.8.97	2979	31S	D-ADBP	DBA	30.12.97	3044	446	JA8998	JAL	25.6.9
2917	3H4	N653SW	SWA	11.8.97	2980	524	N16651	CAL	31.12.97	3045	524	N18658	CAL	25.6.9
2918	3H4	N654SW	SWA	13.8.97	2981	46Q	B-2993	BAS	21.1.98	3046	45R	VT-JAU	Jet	30.6.9
2919	3W0	B-2981	ChYA	21.8.97	2982	31S	D-ADBQ	DBA	15.1.98	3047	36Q	G-OMUC	BAHC	30.6.9
2920	5U3	PK-GGA	Garuda	26.12.97	2983	34S	G-OGBB	GBAir	27.1.98	3048	524	N15659	CAL	30.6.9
2921	36N	N306FL	GECAS	26.8.97	2984	31S	D-ADBR	DBA	23.1.98	3049	4M0	VP-BAJ	Aflot	16.7.9
2922	46Q	B-2987	BAHC	27.8.97	2985	524	N14652	CAL	23.1.98	3050	490	N706AS	AlaskA	10.7.9
2923	36Q	D-ADBK	BAS	29.8.97	2986	524	N14653	CAL	27.1.98	3051	4M0	VP-BAL	Aflot	17.7.9
2924	524	N17640	CAL	26.8.97	2987	36N	OO-VEG	GECAS	4.2.98	3052	524	N14660	CAL	15.7.9

Line No	Type No	First Owner Reg	First Owner	Delivery
053	39P	B-2571	CEA	28.7.98
054	35N	B-2995	ShA	30.7.98
055	524	N23661	CAL	21.7.98
056	4M0	VP-BAM	Aflot	28.7.98
057	36Q	ZK-NGC	BAHC	4.8.98
058	4M0	VP-BAN	Aflot	10.8.98
059	3S3	N244SR	SunAC	13.8.98
060	524	N14662	CAL	3.8.98
061	3S3	PP-VPZ	SunAC	17.9.98
062	33V	G-EZYG	EasyJ	19.8.98
063	524	N17663	CAL	11.8.98
064	3U3	N1799B	Boeing	
065	35N	B-2996	ShA	4.9.98
066	524	N14664	CAL	20.8.98
067	44P	B-2501	ChHA	3.9.98
068	5L9	OY-APP	MskA	31.8.98
069	524	N13665	CAL	31.8.98
070	31S	D-ADBT	DBA	17.9.98
071	39P	B-2572	CEA	25.9.98
072	33V	G-EZYH	EasyJ	8.9.98
073	31S	D-ADBU	DBA	30.9.98
074	524	N13666	CAL	30.9.98
075	54K	JA305K	Nippon	15.10.98
076	5L9	OY-APR	MskA	22.10.98
077	524	N14667	CAL	14.10.98
078	4M0	VP-BAO	Aflot	
079	3U3	N1026G	Boeing	
080	39P	B-2573	CEA	
081	4M0	VP-BAP	Aflot	
082	36N	G-IGOJ	GECAS	
083	53S	F-GJNS	PemCC	
084	33V	G-EZYI	EasyJ	
085	4Q3	JA8938	JTA	
086	53S	F-GJNT	PemCC	
087	4M0	VP-BAQ	Aflot	
088	4Q3	JA8939	JTA	
089	33V	G-EZYJ	EasyJ	
091	4M0	VP-BAR	Aflot	
092	31S	D-ADBV	DBA	
093	31S	D-ADBW	DBA	

Boeing 600/700/800 Index

Line No	Type No	First Owner Reg	First Owner	Delivery
1	7H4	N707SA	SWA	30.10.98
2	7H4	N708SW	SWA	
3	7H4	N709SW	SWA	26.10.98
4	7H4	N700GS	SWA	17.12.95
5	75B	D-AGEL	Ger	
6	7H4	N701GS	SWA	19.12.97
7	8K5	D-AHFA	HL	
8	8K5	D-AHFB	HL	
9	8K5	D-AHFC	HL	22.4.98
10	7L9	OY-MRA	MskA	2.3.98
11	7L9	OY-MRB	MskA	6.3.98
12	7H4	N703SW	SWA	31.12.97
13	75B	D-AGEM	Ger	10.3.98
14	7Q8	HB-IIH	ILFC	25.3.98
15	7H4	N704SW	SWA	9.1.98
16	75B	D-AGEN	Ger	
17	75B	D-AGEO	Ger	23.4.98
18	75B	D-AGEP	Ger	21.3.98
19	7K9	N100UN	BFlug	
20	7H4	N705SW	SWA	30.3.98
21	683	SE-DNR	SAS	
22	7Q8	N801LF	ILFC	24.5.98
23	75B	D-AGEQ	Ger	31.7.98
24	7H4	N706SW	SWA	31.5.98
25	7K9	N101UN	BFlug	12.6.98
26	7L9	OY-MRC	MskA	25.5.98
27	75B	D-AGER	Ger	10.6.98
28	75B	D-AGES	Ger	30.6.98
29	724	N16701	CAL	30.3.98
30	75B	D-AGET	Ger	23.3.98
31	75B	D-AGET	Ger	23.3.98
32	724	N24702	CAL	31.3.98
33	705	LN-TUA	Braa	13.4.98
34	7H4	N710SW	SWA	28.3.98
35	7Q8	N301LF	ILFC	5.4.98
36	86J	D-ABAN	ABer	7.5.98
37	724	N16703	CAL	7.4.98
38	7H4	N711HK	SWA	10.4.98

Line No	Type No	First Owner Reg	First Owner	Delivery
39	75B	D-AGEU	Ger	11.4.98
40	8K5	D-AHFD	HL	24.4.98
41	7AD	N700EW	EWA	13/5/98
42	86J	D-ABAO	ABer	
43	724	N14704	CAL	27.4.98
44	8K5	D-AHFE	HL	13.5.98
45	8K5	D-AHFF	HL	16.5.98
46	724	N25705	CAL	12.5.98
47	724	N24706	CAL	26.5.98
48	724	N23707	CAL	27.5.98
49	683	SE-DNM	SAS	18.9.98
50	8Q8	OY-SEA	ILFC	
51	8K2	PH-HZA	TransA	16.6.98
52	724	N23708	CAL	1.6.98
53	7H4	N712SW	SWA	31.5.98
54	7H4	N713SW	SWA	8.6.98
55	8B6	CN-RNJ	RAMar	10.7.98
56	824	N26210	CAL	23.6.98
57	8K2	PH-HZB	TransA	18.6.98
58	824	N24211	CAL	30.6.98
59	8K5	D-AHFG	HL	24.6.98
60	8B6	CN-RNK	RAMar	15.7.98
61	7H4	N714CB	SWA	20.6.98
62	7H4	N715SW	SWA	30.6.98l
63	824	N24212	CAL	30.6.98
64	7H4	N716SW	SWA	30.6.98
65	824	N27213	CAL	14.7.98
66	75B	D-AGEV	Ger	30.6.98
67	86N	N574GE	GECAS	29.7.98
68	75B	D-AGEW	Ger	10.7.98
69	8Z9	OE-LNJ	Lauda	28.7.98
70	7H4	N717SA	SWA	23.7.98
71	7H4	N718SW	SWA	31.7.98
72	7AD	N701EW	EWA	28.7.98
73	75C	B-2998	ChXA	21.8.98
74	824	N14214	CAL	24.7.98
75	8Q8	N800NA	ILFC	2.8.98
76	824	N26215	CAL	4.8.98
77	8Q8	G-OKDN	ILFC	27.7.98
78	8Q8	OY-SEB	ILFC	30.7.98

BELOW: Luton-based easyJet is Britain's first low-cost/no-frills airline.

Line No	Type No	First Owner Reg	First Owner	Delivery
79	824	N12216	CAL	4.8.98
80	8F2	TC-JFC	THY	30.10.98
81	824	N16217	CAL	31.7.98
82	7H4	N719SW	SWA	5.8.98
83	705	LN-TUB	Braa	25.8.98
84	824	N12218	CAL	14.8.98
85	8K2	PH-HZC	TransA	26.8.98
86	75C	B-2999	ChXA	27.8.98
87	8F2	TC-JFD	THY	30.10.98
88	824	N14219	CAL	27.8.98
89	86N	N587GE	GECAS	28.8.98
90	75C	B-2991	ChXA	2.9.98
91	86N	N575GE	GECAS	10.9.98
92	683	OY-KKA	SAS	30.9.98
93	724	N16709	CAL	31.8.98
94	724	N15710	CAL	31.8.98
95	8F2	TC-JFE	THY	30.10.98
96	7X2	DQ-FJF	APac	22.9.98
97	724	N54711	CAL	18.9.98
98	73S	N102UN	PemCC	
99	8F2	TC-JFF	THY	30.10.98
100	683	LN-RPA	SAS	10.10.98
101	73Q	N737BZ (poss)		
102	8F2	TC-JFG	THY	30.10.98
103	86N	N576GE	GECAS	30.9.98
104	73S	N103UN	PemCC	
105	724	N15712	CAL	24.9.98
106	86J	D-ABAP	ABer	6.10.98
107	724	N16713	CAL	24.9.98
108	75C	B-2992	ChXA	29/9/98
109	705	LN-TUC	Braa	25.9.98
110	79K	B-2633	ShenA	30.9.98
111	79U	N1779B	Boeing	23.9.98
112	683	SE-DNN	SAS	21.10.98
113	809	B-18601	ChinA	26.10.98
114	8F2	TC-JFH	THY	30.10.98
115	832	N371DA	Delta	22.10.98
116	683	SE-DNO	SAS	19.10.98
117	809	B-18602	ChinA	29.10.98
118	832	N372DA	Delta	26.10.98
119	724	N33714	CAL	28.9.98
120	683	OY-KKB	SAS	
121	7H4	N720WN	SWA	30.9.98
122	7Q8	B-2632	ILFC	9.10.98
123	832	N373DA	Delta	27.10.98
124	86N	N577GE	GECAS	30.10.98
125	724	N24715	CAL	21.10.98
126	75V	N366G	GE	20.11.98;
127	79K	B-2635	ShenA	20.10.98
128	832	N374DA	Delta	
129	809	B-18603	ChinA	
130	809	B-18605	ChinA	
131	72T	N50TC	Boeing	20.11.98
132	809	B-18606	ChinA	
133	86J	D-ABAQ	ABer	24.10.98
134	824	N18220	CAL	
135	76N	PP-VQA	GECAS	
136	7L9	OY-MRD	MskA	
137	683	LN-RPB	SAS	15.11.98
139	809	B-18607	ChinA	
140	7W0	B-2639	ChYA	
143	73T	N1787B	Boeing	
144	7H4	N739GB	SWA	12.11.98

Line No	Type No	First Owner Reg	First Owner	Delivery
146	72U	N1787B	Boeing	
148	7W0	B-2640	ChYA	
151	85F	F-GRNC	GATX	
153	834	N12221	CAL	
155	7H4	N740SW	SWA	
156	724	N13716	CAL	
157	7H4	N741SA	SWA	
158	75U	N1786B	Boeing	
159	834	N34222	CAL	
	683	LN-RPC	SAS	
	683	LN-RPD	SAS	
	683	OY-KKC	SAS	
	683	OY-KKD	SAS	
	683	SE-DNP	SAS	
	683	SE-DNS	SAS	
	683	SE-DNT	SAS	
	683	SE-DNU	SAS	
	683	SE-DNX	SAS	
	705	LN-TUD	Braa	
	705	LN-TUE	Braa	
	705	LN-TUF	Braa	
	705	LN-TUG	Braa	
	724	N13718	CAL	
	724	N14725	CAL	
	724	N14731	CAL	
	724	N16732	CAL	
	724	N17320	CAL	
	724	N17719	CAL	
	724	N17730	CAL	
	724	N21723	CAL	
	724	N23721	CAL	
	724	N24729	CAL	
	724	N27722	CAL	
	724	N27723	CAL	
	724	N27724	CAL	
	724	N27734	CAL	
	724	N29717	CAL	
	724	N38727	CAL	
	724	N39726	CAL	
	724	N39728	CAL	
	724	N49725	CAL	
	7H4	N723SW	SWA	
	7H4	N724SW	SWA	
	7H4	N725SW	SWA	
	7H4	N726SW	SWA	
	7H4	N727SW	SWA	
	7H4	N728SW	SWA	
	7H4	N729SW	SWA	
	7H4	N730SW	SWA	
	7H4	N731SA	SWA	
	7H4	N732SW	SWA	
	7H4	N733SA	SWA	
	7H4	N734SA	SWA	
	7H4	N735SA	SWA	
	7H4	N736SA	SWA	
	7H4	N737JW	SWA	
	7H4	N738CB	SWA	
	7H4	N742SW	SWA	
	7H4	N743SW	SWA	
	7H4	N744SW	SWA	
	7H4	N745SW	SWA	
	7H4	N746SW	SWA	
	7H4	N747SA	SWA	

Line No	Type No	First Owner Reg	First Owner	Delive
	7H4	N748SW	SWA	
	7H4	N749SW	SWA	
	7H4	N750SA	SWA	
	7H4	N751SW	SWA	
	7H4	N752SW	SWA	
	7L9	OY-MRE	MskA	
	7L9	OY-MRF	MskA	
	85F	F-GRNA	GATX	
	85R	VT-JNC	Jet	
	85R	VT-JND	Jet	
	86J	D-ABAR	ABer	
	86J	D-ABAS	ABer	
	86J	D-ABAT	ABer	
	86J	D-ABAU	ABer	
	8K2	PH-HZD	TransA	
	8K2	PH-HZE	TransA	
	8K2	PH-HZG	TransA	
	8K5	D-AHFH	HL	
	8K5	D-AHFI	HL	
	8K5	D-AHFJ	HL	
	8K5	D-AHFK	HL	
	8X2	DQ-FJG	APac	
	8X2	DQ-FJH	APac	
	806	PH-BXA	KLM	
	806	PH-BXB	KLM	
	806	PH-BXC	KLM	
	806	PH-BXD	KLM	
	809	B-18608	ChinA	
	809	B-18609	ChinA	
	809	B-18610	ChinA	
	809	B-18611	ChinA	
	823	N901AN	AA	
	823	N902AN	AA	
	823	N903AN	AA	
	823	N904AN	AA	
	823	N905AN	AA	
	823	N906AN	AA	
	823	N907AN	AA	
	823	N908AN	AA	
	823	N909AM	AA	
	823	N910AN	AA	
	823	N912AN	AA	
	823	N913AN	AA	
	824	N18223	CAL	
	832	N375DA	Delta	
	832	N376DA	Delta	
	832	N378DA	Delta	
	832	N379DA	Delta	
	858	4X-EKA	El Al	
	858	4X-EKB	El Al	
	858	4X-EKC	El Al	
	858	4X-EKD	El Al	
	858	4X-EKE	El Al	

RIGHT: At the end of the day — a United Airlines Boeing 737-300 about to touchdown on runway 25L at its Los Angeles base.

9 CHRONOLOGY

19 Feb 1965	737 launch announced, Lufthansa order.
5 April 1965	United Airline orders the type -200.
9 April 1967	First flight of 737-100.
8 Aug 1967	First flight of 737-200.
Dec 1967	First 737 delivered (to Lufthansa).
10 Feb 1968	B737-100 enters service with Lufthansa.
28 Aug 1968	B737-200 enters service with United.
Sept 1968	First flight of -200QC variant.
March 1981	Series -300 launch announced.
April 1982	Sale of 1,000th 737 announced.
24 Feb 1984	First flight of 737-300.
4 June 1986	Series -400 launch announced.
20 May 1987	Series -500 launch announced.
19 Feb 1988	First flight of 737-400.
Aug 1988	1,114th and last -200 delivered.
30 June 1989	First flight of 737-500.
19 Feb 1990	Best selling airliner – 1,833rd rolled out.
28 Feb 1990	First -500 delivered (Southwest).
25 Feb 1991	2,000th 737 delivered (100th for Lufthansa).
16 Oct 1991	1,000th New Generation 737 delivered (-400 for British Airways).
17 Nov 1993	Next Generation 737 programme launched as the 737X — later to be called the series -600, -700 and -800.
Jan 1994	Southwest Airlines orders 63 series -700 to become launch customer.
July 1994	Maersk Air becomes European launch customer for the -700 with orders for 6 planes.
Nov 1994	Hapag-Lloyd order 16 series -800s for delivery early 1998, thus becoming launch customer.
2 July 1996	Boeing Business Jets formed in a joint venture with General Electric.
Nov 1996	American announces massive order, including 75 -800s for delivery between 1998 and 2001.
21 Nov 1996	501 Next Generation 737s on are on order.
8 Dec 1996	First Next Generation 737, a series -700 rolled out. (2,843rd 737 built).
31 Dec 1996	449 737s were ordered during 1996. Total 737 orders now 3,604 with 2,840 delivered.

Feb 1997	First flight of the 737-700.
7 Feb 1997	-700 sets 737 altitude record —41,000ft (12,500m).
0 June 1997	Roll out of first 737-800.
1 July 1997	First flight of the 737-800.
Autumn 1997	Southwest takes delivery of its last (186th) -300.
Oct 1997	Delivery of first 737-700 to Southwest Airlines.
Nov 1997	-700 certification by the JAA.
0 Nov 1997	Boeing announces the launch of the -900. Alaskan is launch customer with order for 10.
Dec 1997	Roll out of first 737-600.
2 Jan 1998	First flight of 737-600.

TOP: Russian independent operator Transaero has acquired two 737-700s leased from Bavaria to augment its fleet of elderly -200s. The new type is used on the Moscow–London/Gatwick route. This is 737-7K9 N100UN delivered April 1998.

ABOVE: Sabre Airways is the only British operator of Next Generation 737s — two 737-8Q8s. The first, G-OKDN was delivered on 27 July 1998 and is seen here at Gatwick. These aircraft operate non-stop Gatwick–Banjul in West Africa.

BELOW LEFT: Seen awaiting delivery is 737-7H4 N709SW. This is the third -700 built, and the third for launch customer Southwest. The first batch of this variant for the airline was delayed due to late certification of the type.

19 Feb 1998	European certification for the 737-800.
March 1998	Delivery of first 737-800 to launch customer Hapag-Lloyd.
13 March 1998	US FAA grant type certification to the -800 for passenger service within the US.
18 Aug 1998	FAA granted type certification to the Next Generation 737-600.
18 Sept 1998	Launch customer SAS took delivery of the first of their 55 orders for -600s.

INDEX

BELOW: German charter operators were early customers for Next Generation 737s. Here Hapag-Lloyd's 737-8K5 D-AHFG is seen about to depart Lanzarote.